HOW TO BUY
THE RIGHT INSURANCE
AT THE RIGHT PRICE

OTHER ONE HOUR GUIDES

Bailard, Biehl & Kaiser:	How to Set and Achieve Your Financial Goals
	How to Be a Successful Investor
Tauber:	How to Retire Young
Thomsett:	How to Sell Your Home for Top Dollar

HOW TO BUY
THE RIGHT INSURANCE
AT THE RIGHT PRICE

Bailard, Biehl & Kaiser, Inc.

Dow Jones-Irwin
Homewood, Illinois 60430

Project editor: Gladys True
Production mananger: Ann Cassady
Cover design: Image House
Cover illustration: David Lesh
Compositor: Precision Typographers
Typeface: 10/12 Souvenir Light
Printer: Arcata Graphics/Kingsport

Library of Congress Cataloging-in-Publication Data

Bailard, Thomas E.
    How to buy the right insurance at the right price / Thomas E.
  Bailard, David L. Biehl, Ronald W. Kaiser.
        p.   cm.
    Includes index.
    ISBN 1-55623-146-6
    1. Insurance—United States.   I. Biehl, David L.   II. Kaiser,
Ronald W.   III.   Title.
HG8951.B34   1989   89-1221
368'.0029—dc19   CIP

Printed in the United States of America
1 2 3 4 5 6 7 8 9 0   K   6 5 4 3 2 1 0 9

PREFACE

It is shocking to hear that approximately 80 percent of Americans buy the wrong kind of insurance for their particular needs. When you stop to think about it, that's far more frightening than the threat of loss in the first place. Being inaccurately insured is like walking in the forest blindfolded—you not only run a high risk of getting banged up; there are no bandages available when it happens.

How to Buy the Right Insurance at the Right Price will help you learn everything you really need to know about protecting yourself, your family, and your every possession. We can almost guarantee that you won't want to skip pages once you discover how valuable this information will be to you all the rest of your life. We've made it easy and fun. Nowhere on the bookstands will you find a book like this. The insurance companies won't be pleased, but we think you'll enjoy using it, and we know you'll be glad to own it.

The information in this book and others in the series has been developed during our years of experience as financial advisors. We have helped hundreds of clients achieve their goals using the methods we describe in these pages. These goals have been as varied as the people themselves. They include achieving financial independence, traveling the world, paying for higher education, providing for a family's financial security in retirement years, and many others.

Our popular seminars on personal money management have helped thousands of people—entrepreneurs, corporate executives, recent college graduates, and retirees—become true *money managers*. They learned the importance of moving beyond being mere money makers and money spenders in order to achieve their life's goals.

Our college textbook, *Personal Money Management* (published by Science Research Associates and now in its fifth edition) is the leading text in its field. Hundreds of thousands of university and continuing education students have learned the fundamentals of personal finance through the book.

Our own entrepreneurial experience that ranges from our days together at Stanford Graduate School of Business to the top management of our own diversified corporation has convinced us personally of the wisdom of these techniques. We offer no advice nor suggest any course of action that we have not applied successfully ourselves.

For many years this hard-won expertise was available only to wealthy investors and institutional accounts who could afford our specialized services and who could appreciate the value of objective financial advice. Clients like these demand not only successful track records, but also a deeper understanding of the role of money in achieving career and life goals. It was from our desire to make such counsel available to more people that this book and series were born.

Of course any publication owes its success to many people behind the scenes. In addition to the generous cooperation of our clients, without whose feedback and support this series would not have been possible, we especially wish to thank Jerrold D. Dickson for his ideas and presentation of the BB&K approach to setting and achieving your financial goals; Jeri Hayes for her personal high standards in editing this work; and Brenda Locke for her organizational abilities in seeing this project through to completion.

To these and many others who helped us create, prepare, and deliver this book, we express our sincerest gratitude. With them, we take great pride and pleasure in welcoming you to our growing family of clients.

Thomas E. Bailard
David L. Biehl
Ronald W. Kaiser

CONTENTS

1. INTRODUCTION   1

Why Should You Learn About Insurance?

> Proper Insurance Coverage Is Crucial to Financial Success. A Simple Concept Made Complex. You Become the Expert.

2. INSURANCE PRINCIPLES   4

Insurable Risks:

> Historical Development. Dealing with Insurable Risks. Making the Insurance Decision Yourself. What to Insure. What to Insure Against. How Much to Insure For. How Long to Keep Your Insurance.

How to Buy a Policy:

> Dealing with Insurance Agents. The Insurance Policy.

Wrapping Up.

3. COMPREHENSIVE LIABILITY AND AUTO INSURANCE   18

Liability and You:

> Four Types of Liability Exposure. Determining the Amount of Coverage You Need.

General Liability Coverage:

> Jacket Provisions. Coverage Provisions. Umbrella Liability Policies.

The Need for Auto Insurance:

> Jacket and Coverage Provisions. Fitting Coverage to Your Needs.

Insurance Rates: Ups, Downs, and Ways Around:

> Age and Rates. Other Variables. Assigned Risk Plans. Shopping Around.

After An Auto Accident:

> Making a Claim. Sizing Up the Damages.

Wrapping Up.

4. PROPERTY INSURANCE   40

What Property Can Be Insured?

The Role of Property Insurance. Market Value versus Replacement
Cost.

Determining What You Own and Its Value:

Taking a Personal Property Inventory. Valuing Your Home.

Finding the Right Type of Insurance Coverage:

Homeowners Policies. Flood and Earthquake Insurance.
Understanding the Fine Print. Making a Claim. Money-Saving Tips.

Wrapping Up.

5. HEALTH INSURANCE   58

Determining Your Medical Insurance Needs:

Prepayment and Indemnity Plans. Types of Medical Plans.

Disability Income Needs:

Self-Insuring for Income Loss. Other Types of Income Loss Protection.
Determining Your Disability Needs. What to Look for When Buying
Disability Coverage. Understanding the Clauses in Disability Insurance.

Group Health Insurance:

Duplication of Coverage. Shopping for the Best Values.

Workers Compensation.

Wrapping Up.

6. LIFE INSURANCE   81

Determining Your Life Insurance Needs:

An Eight-Step Approach. Decreasing Needs and Increasing Assets.

Variables in Life Insurance Policies:

Term Insurance: Pure Insurance. Cash Value Insurance. Deciding
Which to Buy: Term or Cash Value? Watching Out for Those Contract
Clauses. Customizing the Policy to Fit Your Needs. Settlement
Options. The Need for Comparison Shopping.

Wrapping Up.

7. END PAPER   108

Who Are You?

Slaying Your Emotional Dragons. The Bottom Line. What Are You?
Actions Speak Louder. Evaluating Your Control-Taking Style.
Property: What Does It Mean to You? Replacement Value. Evaluating
Your Social Needs Profile.

Wrapping Up.

APPENDIX: ACTION PAPERS   123

INDEX   131

CHAPTER 1

INTRODUCTION

WHY SHOULD YOU LEARN ABOUT INSURANCE?

Insurance. The very term stirs unpleasant thoughts for many people. No one wants to think about the things that can go wrong in life. But the unfortunate fact is that life is filled with aggravating and often expensive surprises. And too often, it is only after the fact that people discover their need for insurance.

Studies show that some 80 percent of all Americans are either underinsured, overinsured, or simply have the wrong insurance for their needs. The same people who carefully evaluate and monitor each investment dollar all too often take a less disciplined approach to buying insurance. The reasons for this are easy to understand. Insurance is certainly not as sexy as investing. Few people exchange insurance tips at a cocktail party!

Proper Insurance Coverage Is Crucial to Financial Success

Yet your insurance purchases can prove every bit as important to your financial well-being as your stock, bond, or real estate decisions. Being inadequately insured is dangerous to you and your family's future. In today's litigious society a minor fender-bender auto accident can result in a very expensive lawsuit. A serious illness that requires hospitalization can run up thousands of dollars in bills over a very short time. Extended disability can devastate your family's finances.

If you do not have the proper insurance coverage, these events can cause virtually irreparable harm to your financial future. Our goal with this book is to help you sort through the maze of data that is available, and to focus on those kernels of information you really need to know to protect yourself, your family, and your possessions.

1

A Simple Concept Made Complex

Insurance can be a dense and frightful subject. Making an incorrect purchase is not only possible, it is all too common. When you make an incorrect purchase, you probably will not discover this until after you need to make a claim. If your house has already burned to the ground, your car stolen, or your home burglarized, it is too late to find out that you have purchased the wrong coverage.

There are a number of reasons that insurance seems so complicated. It has its own confusing terminology. Different types of insurance are designed for different types of risks. Your own protection objectives are often complicated. Insurance sales agents do not always offer the most objective information. Some tend to sell policies rather than the needed benefits for their clients.

Our research shows that there is a desperate need for the type of book we have written here. Our goal is to clarify and simplify the subject for you. Once you understand the underlying principles of insurance, you won't be intimidated by the jumble of often misleading marketing jargon that characterizes the field.

Insurance is a natural extension of our desire to protect what is ours. At first we are only concerned with guarding our health and property. When we begin a family, we first realize the need to make provisions for those who depend on us financially.

Once you have built that foundation—a job, a home, a family—you need to take measures to ensure that you and your family won't lose the necessities of life—food, clothing, shelter—as a result of an accident or illness. Without that protection, the personal and financial goals you are working toward can be rendered totally out of reach.

For centuries, people have developed different methods for coping with future uncertainties. It is a little more formal and certainly more complicated these days, but the goals are essentially the same.

You Become the Expert

We've designed this book to be an interactive exercise to maximize its benefits for your particular circumstances. First, we explain what's behind all that insurance jargon. Chapter 2 introduces basic insurance principles. What follows is a detailed discussion of the various types of insurance. You'll complete a personal inventory and prioritize your insurance needs.

Heading that priority list, you decide what you really need to insure, against what, for how much, for how long, and finally, where to buy the policy. You will also learn how to prepare for and handle claims, just in case.

Just as the same investment is not appropriate for all investors, neither is the same coverage appropriate for all people. In fact, it is critical that you tailor your insurance coverage to meet your current needs. That is why it is important to find out about yourself as you will do at the end of this book.

By the time you finish this book, you can map out a protection plan that is tailored specifically for you. You will know how to spend your protection dollars most effectively. You will be well on your way to achieving your own peace of mind.

CHAPTER 2

INSURANCE PRINCIPLES

There are many misconceptions about insurance. Some of these result from advertising excesses on the part of insurance companies. Often people are influenced to buy certain types of policies such as cancer insurance, rather than buying the benefits such as the payment of medical bills, that an insurance policy should provide.

The picture becomes even more confusing when the consumer is confronted with a bewildering assortment of clauses, exclusions, endorsements, and other minutiae. The financial services revolution has affected more than banks and savings institutions over the past ten years. Insurance products have become even more confusing as the industry rolls out ever more variations.

In this chapter we cut through the dense underbrush of confusing details and focus on the broad picture. You will learn what insurance is, what it is for, how much you should buy, when you should buy, and how long you should hold onto it. Once you have determined what you want, you will have to buy from someone. We conclude the chapter with notes on selecting an insurance provider and working with a sales agent.

INSURABLE RISKS

Insurance is a device that protects against life's adverse contingencies—those events you hope will never occur. When buying insurance your guiding considerations should be *need* and *practicality*. Being overinsured is not a luxury, it is a waste. Overcautiousness can be downright frivolous when it comes to insurance. How many times have you been tempted by some offer of accidental dismemberment insurance? Does it really make much sense to carry coverage that will pay only if you lose an arm, and double if you lose an arm and a leg?

The first questions you must ask are, "Do I need it?" and "Is it practical?" You are protecting yourself from something you hope never occurs. In fact, in most circumstances, the best thing that can happen is that your premium payments are lost money. You win when you don't get a material return on your investment. The psychological return of peace of mind is difficult to quantify.

That is the difference between *insurance* protection and *nest egg* protection. With a nest egg, you hope your investment grows and contributes to your prosperity. Pure insurance doesn't grow. It is not designed to help you make money. (Certain forms of life insurance are sold as investments, but these policies are actually hybrids in which part of the money is set aside strictly for insurance purposes. The balance is invested. The insurance portion is a nonrecoverable.)

Insurance will only replace with dollars what was measurable in dollars in the first place, was lost due to bad luck, and was personal in origin. If any one of these factors is missing, then insurance is not applicable.

For example, insurance does not cover losses that occur as a result of deliberate action on the part of the insured. You can't take a baseball bat to your car windows and then expect to collect damages. You cannot leave the keys in your car and encourage people to steal it, then expect to recover the value of your car from your insurance company.

Insurance can't bring back friends or relatives. It can't rescue that favorite reading chair. It can't give you back your perfect heart after triple bypass surgery. These things are not measurable in dollars.

Finally, insurance will not cover losses from risks that affect large numbers of people all at once—such as war or revolution—rather than individuals being affected randomly. These simple concepts are the core of understanding insurance. They also explain what insurance companies do once a claim is filed. They investigate claims to determine the causes of financial losses before making payments.

Historical Development

In 1825 a committee of the House of Commons in England was asked to explain the principle of insurance when reporting on the laws relating to friendly societies. Following is what the committee said:

> Whenever there is a contingency, the cheapest way of providing against it is by uniting with others, so that each man may subject himself to a small deprivation, in order that no man may be subjected to a great loss. He, upon whom the contingency does not fall, does not get his money back again, nor does he get it for any visible or tangible benefit; but he obtains security against ruin and consequent peace of mind. He, upon whom the contingency does fall, gets all that

those, whom fortune has exempted from it, have lost in hard money, and is thus enabled to sustain an event which would otherwise overwhelm him.

Even 160 years ago, the same insurance principles were understood and practiced. While there are many reasons that people buy insurance, the most important is protection against financial disaster. Whether it is 160 years ago or today, that goal should be uppermost in the buyer's mind.

Dealing with Insurable Risks

There are three ways you can deal with insurable risks: *minimize, retain*, or *transfer*. The exact mix you choose will depend in large part on your psychological makeup (how well you handle risk and cope with losses), your financial status (how much of a loss you could sustain without affecting your lifestyle) and your family status (how many people are dependent on you).

You can minimize insurable risks by choosing different courses of action. For example, staying off the ski slopes will lower the risk of leg injuries. Skipping hang gliding will lower the risk of broken bones. Forgoing a game of Russian roulette will lower your odds of dying. This approach can be taken to absurd extremes. Locking yourself inside and leaving only to buy groceries at the corner store will minimize many risks. It will also be extremely boring!

You probably have heard the term *self-insured*. Many large corporations self-insure certain types of risk. Rather than pay a premium to an insurance company, the corporation decides for one reason or another that the best approach is to be prepared to pay claims from its own resources. When you elect a $500 deductible on your auto policy, you are self-insuring for that amount because it comes out of your pocket if a loss occurs.

But in today's litigation-crazed world, this alternative for individuals is becoming less and less viable. If you have sufficient assets to meet most judgments, it still does not make sense to risk losing them through a liability lawsuit. Some wealthy individuals maintain insurance to protect themselves from lawsuits, but self-insure their own property. If you have sufficient assets to replace what can be stolen without adversely affecting your lifestyle, this approach may make sense. But in some areas, especially health and liability, self-insurance is a losing proposition for most.

The most common way to insure is to transfer the risk to a third party. This approach was outlined in our historical example above. An insurance company assumes the risks for its policyholders. The company's underwriters study many things such as prices and odds of occurrences, and set a premium rate. Policyholders pool their funds with the company. As long as the company's losses do not exceed its premium income, it makes money. If losses start to exceed premium income, rates will rise until the company recovers its costs.

Making the Insurance Decision Yourself

Determining the appropriate amount of insurance coverage for your needs starts with a simple mathematical exercise. Begin with a review of your balance sheet and income statement. You will quickly find your asset of greatest value. It is probably your home (if you own it), your car, or maybe even your income stream if you have a good job but either have not had time to accumulate tangible assets or are not interested in owning more things.

Don't take for granted that what is appropriate insurance for others or even for most people is what you need. Here is where your insurance planning begins. For example, if worldwide travel is your highest priority rather than, for example, raising a family or building a career, your insurance needs will be far different from those of other people. You will need to secure appropriate coverage for your health and the wherewithal for lots of airline tickets. Of course, this assumes you have found a way to secure your cash flow!

Once you have reappraised what is important to you, consider the following questions:

1. What would happen if your assets were substantially diminished (e.g., your home is destroyed or you become unemployed)?
2. If driving is a comfort or necessity in your life, would you need $2,500 or $25,000 to replace your car if it were stolen?
3. How much would your family need to meet expenses if you were disabled or died?
4. If someone fell down your poorly lighted front steps after a rollicking party, broke a leg, and sued you for negligence to the tune of $20,000, could you cover it? Remember, even if you win a suit such as this there can be very high legal bills.

What to Insure

How do you decide what to insure? The following guidelines suggest some ways to sensibly protect yourself. Remember, your goal is to get the most protection at a reasonable price. It does not make sense to secure protection for virtually every possible contingency by paying out all your cash flow!

1. Your insurance goal is to protect yourself from major financial disasters. Don't be concerned about protecting every last dime. Distinguish whether you are guarding against something that would cause you or your loved ones serious dollar loss, or whether you are making a prepayment for something you are pretty sure will happen such as college expenses for your child. You may be able to prepare for the latter less expensively and more effectively with a specific investment vehicle.

2. You must set priorities. Insurance is going to cost money. Separate those things that must be insured for your peace of mind, from those things that should be insured if you can afford it. And finally, list those things that you might insure for fuller protection. You will find that as your circumstances change over time, so will your insurance needs. Some of the items in your "should" or even "might" lists may be affordable or may change to "musts" when you review them in the future.

What to Insure Against

An old Wall Street saw notes that "Forecasting is difficult, especially about the future." But while forecasts of tomorrow's interest rates, stocks prices, or weather have a large element of uncertainty, there are some things you value for sure. Once you have determined what you want to insure, you will need to know what hazards threaten them. Here are some tips on coverage of various perils:

1. Know the order in which you would rank loss of life, income, health, and property. These rankings will vary from person to person depending on lifestyle, value systems, and financial condition.

2. Insurance companies analyze a vast amount of data to assess the probability of repeat occurrences. For example, they examine the number of burglary cases or auto accidents that occur in a given time period in a specific place. They then categorize this data into equal-risk groups. For example, since studies show that vandalism and theft tend to occur with roughly equal frequency, they are grouped under a single-peril category. Because of this practice, you will often find that in order to get the coverage you need, you may have to buy coverage on something you don't really need. For example, if you live on a farm you may want to protect against theft of your equipment. However, to get that coverage you may have to pay for protection against vandalism, a very unlikely occurrence.

3. Logically enough, the broader the coverage the costlier the premium. It pays to ask questions. Policies vary widely. Don't feel you must buy the first policy suggested to you. Make sure the policy you buy fits your requirements, not the salesperson's.

Initially, you may have to settle for less than perfect coverage. But with the highly competitive insurance industry, there is a good chance something better may come along by the time you next review your insurance needs.

How Much to Insure For

It is fairly easy to determine the value of your personal property. Assessing the financial effect of your death on those left behind is considerably more difficult. We cover this issue in Chapter 6.

As we mentioned above, you can self-insure by selecting a deductible on your policy. For example, if your policy has a $100 deductible, you will pay the first $100 of a loss. Your insurance company will pay the balance up to the limits of the policy. A higher deductible lowers the premium you have to pay.

However, unless you also set aside an emergency fund to cover the potential losses, you are not self-insuring as much as you are gambling! Before you determine the deductible, you must decide whether you have the means and discipline to set aside an amount equal to the deductible.

You should carefully consider the deductible clause on your auto insurance. Factors to weigh include the age of your car (your insurance will only pay the current value of your car, not what you paid for it), your previous loss record (a fenderbender or a total loss), how much you drive, whether you drink, what types of roads you drive on, and so forth. You will find that changing your deductible can make a significant difference in your premium.

The same principle applies to health insurance. If you break a leg on the slopes every year or are inclined to daydream when crossing the street, a small deductible may be the way to go. In fact, if you engage in fairly dangerous sports—skiing, hang gliding, parachuting, football—you should consider maintaining a low deductible. Your personal loss experience is your best guide to selecting the appropriate deductible.

You should consider taking the money saved from the lower premiums you are required to pay for higher deductible policies and putting it into a high interest-bearing investment. You may actually make some money in the bargain. However, if you choose the higher deductible route and then spend the reserved funds, you may just be increasing your financial risk.

As we said at the beginning, insurance is very personal. Only you can be the judge. You determine what you need by knowing who you are.

Over the years we have found that a simple calculation is valuable for helping determine the proper deductible. We call this formula the "BB&K Rule-of-Three." Our method says that if dividing the premium saving into the increase in the deductible results in a quotient three or fewer, take the higher deductible. Do the calculation for the full range of deductibles until you find the lowest number.

For example, assume that the premium on your current policy is $500 with a $100 deductible. When it comes time for renewal, you decide to look into the possibility of lowering your premium costs by taking a higher deductible. Table 2-1 illustrates how to compare these alternatives.

The top row of figures reflects your current policy: $500 premium with a $100 deductible. If you raise your deductible to $250, the premium would drop to $400. Using our formula, you would divide the $150 additional deductible amount by the $100 you would save in the premium. Your added savings quotient (ASQ) is 1.5.

TABLE 2–1
Premium/Deductible Comparisons

Premium	Deductible		Added Savings Quotient
$500 ⎱ $400 ⎰	$100 ⎱ $250 ⎰	$150 added deductible —————————————— $100 premium savings	= 1.5
$400 ⎱ $200 ⎰	$250 ⎱ $500 ⎰	$250 added deductible —————————————— $200 added premium savings	= 1.25*
$200 ⎱ $100 ⎰	$500 ⎱ $1,000 ⎰	$500 added deductible —————————————— $100 added premium savings	= 5

*Lowest Quotient—choose this one!

You then would see what additional savings would accrue from a further increase in the deductible. The second example in Table 2-1 shows that an increase to a $500 deductible would result in a decline of $200 in the premium ($400 – $200 = $200). In this case, the $250 added deductible ($250 to $500) is divided by the $200 added premium savings to get an ASQ of 1.25.

Since that figure is lower than the 1.5 in the first example, you know that is the preferred option. However, before you know whether it is the optimum alternative, you will need to see what savings would occur on the next increase in deductible that is available. You can see in the third example that the ASQ jumps to 5. That tells you that the best option among those offered here is the $500 deductible with a $200 premium.

How Long to Keep Your Insurance

Most insurance policies are written for one year or less (homeowners, auto, annual renewable term life). It is a good idea to review your policies on their renewal dates to ensure that your coverage is still necessary and appropriate. It certainly makes no sense to carry auto insurance on a car you sold three months ago. You would be surprised how often things like that are overlooked.

Even for policies issued for periods of more than one year, such as health, disability, and many types of life insurance, it is smart to review them annually. Reassess them with these factors in mind:

1. Do the needs being covered still exist? (e.g., Did your 20-year-old son leave home to go to work where he has his own health coverage?)

2. Are the perils covered still important to you (e.g., if you no longer ride a motorcycle, the risk of a motorcycle accident no longer exists.)
3. Is the policy still the most cost-effective way to meet your needs? (e.g., Are there new policies that more accurately meet your needs at lower prices?)

If there is one lesson we want you to remember most clearly from this book, it is that insurance is not something you buy and put away forever. It has a specific time and place depending on your needs. Those needs change constantly throughout your life.

Insurance is for protection from major financial risks. There is no simple formula for the right amount of insurance for everyone. You need just the right amount for you. Your needs change over time. Review your needs periodically and when there is a significant change in your life or lifestyle. The time you spend researching the subject before anything disastrous happens will be certain to pay off if it happens.

HOW TO BUY A POLICY

When buying your insurance you should shop around to find the coverage that suits your needs most closely, the agent with whom you can work most effectively, and the best insurance company offering the most competitive prices for its policies. You can narrow your list of potential contacts by asking friends, attorneys, bankers, or accountants to recommend agents. If you have the time, you may want to check the Yellow Pages of your local telephone directory to get a list of independent agencies in your neighborhood.

The best way to begin is to get rate quotes on similar coverages. You may be surprised by the wide variances in prices for what appears to be comparable coverage. You are looking for the best combination of rates with broad coverage. The intangible consideration is service. Is the agent willing to spend time with you discussing your real needs? Does the agent present you with a single option? Does the agent represent enough different companies to be able to give you a good perspective on the best prices and coverage available?

Once you have narrowed down your choices to a manageable list, you will need to get into the specifics of your personal circumstances. If your particular situation distinguishes you from most people; for example, if you do not smoke, do not collect antique cars, or have had trouble getting insurance coverage in the past; there may be some companies that will have a special offer for you. Also, some companies specialize in types of coverage. For example, they may work exclusively with homeowners insurance for renters, condominium owners, or owners of single-family homes. While sometimes these firms offer well-priced policies that meet specific needs, don't automatically assume that a specialist firm will necessarily offer the best deal for you.

There are a wide variety of coverages available to fit just about every situation. But it does take some exploring to find the ones that are right for you. If you want to get the most cost-effective and high-quality insurance, you will have to shop around and compare prices and special features for the policy or combination of policies that best fits you. Be forewarned: the cheapest insurance is not always the best bargain.

If you are unsure about a company, you can check out its financial standing in *Best's Insurance Guide* at your local library. Look for companies rated either "A" or "A + ." Premiums and coverages vary substantially even among similarly rated companies. The variable for you is your overall personal financial security.

Dealing with Insurance Agents

The relationship with your insurance agent is becoming ever more important as the insurance business becomes increasingly complex. There are so many new products, specialized coverages, discounts, and surcharges being continually added that it is far more than a layperson can keep up with. When you are shopping for your coverage, you are looking for two things: price and service. The relationship you establish with your agent may be the single most important factor in buying and keeping a policy.

Your main concern in selecting an agent should not be the agent's title or even company affiliation, but rather how much this person knows and how much attention will be paid to your concerns. When an agent is trying to sell you a policy or package of policies, listen not just for what the policy will do for you, but for what the person selling it will do after the sale.

Don't be afraid to ask any questions that come to mind. There is no such thing as a dumb question when you are on the buying end. If you do not ask, you are partly to blame for not getting the correct and complete information. No agent is a mind reader.

To find the best product at the best price, you must rely on your agent's interest and responsibility running a close second to your own. You can help secure your agent's long-term financial interest in you by placing all your insurance business through him or her. A good agent should be able to suggest ways to tailor your policies to get the best fit possible within your price constraints.

Agent Types

Agents are classified by the types of insurance they sell. *Property/casualty agents* deal with auto, home, and personal property insurance. In addition to making sales, these agents typically have an *underwriting* role as well. This simply means that they play a role in determining whether the person applying for a policy is a good risk. This influences how much the premium will be when there is a high and low range.

Property/casualty agents own the policyholder's records. This enables them to transfer coverage from one insurance company to another. They have the power to bind (obligate) an insurance company for coverage before the policy is actually issued. This makes it possible for a potential policyholder to become insured instantly. For example, if you just bought a new car, you want to be able to drive it immediately rather than having to wait for a policy to be issued. A call to your agent should be all you need.

The *life/health agent* has fewer underwriting and service responsibilities. The agent determines which company offers appropriate coverage and submits a potential policyholder's application for acceptance or rejection by the company itself. With policies becoming more complicated and competitive, the agent's duties will (or should) follow suit, encouraging more and better service to policyholders.

Independent or Employee

Another way to classify agents is by their relationship to insurance companies. There are three general types of professional insurance agents and advisors:

1. Independent agents are self-employed. They normally represent two or more companies. They are paid on a commission basis for sales and service.
2. Exclusive agents sell for only one company. They are paid by either commission or as salaried employees.
3. Brokers, like independent agents, are licensed by more than one company. They can sell many lines of insurance—property, liability, health, auto, and so on. They work with other agents and companies in arranging appropriate coverage. A good broker effectively shops the market for you.

Most insurance agents are compensated at least in part by commissions. The size of the commission varies depending on the type of insurance and the size of the premium. Some types of policies pay higher commissions than other types. If an agent seems overanxious to sell a particular policy, this may be an explanation. You may want to find another agent.

The Insurance Policy

An insurance policy is a legal contract that spells out exactly what the issuing company will or will not do for you in certain loss situations. There are two kinds of policy provisions: *jacket* and *coverage*. There are usually five jacket provisions:

1. The *general issuing agreement* states that the company agrees to pay the sum that the contract specifies as settlement against claims that are covered.
2. The *supplementary payments* section outlines the expenses, if any, the company will pay in addition to the settlement expense.
3. The *definitions* section defines the common terms relating to the conditions of the coverage.
4. The *conditions* segment details those conditions under which the contract will be considered valid.
5. The *declarations* section identifies who is to be covered against what. The what is determined by the coverage provisions selected by the policyholder.

The coverage provisions are your instructions to the insurance company. By choosing one or more coverage provisions, you tell the insurance company who is to be covered, what injury or property damage is to be covered, and what is not to be covered.

A third element in an insurance policy is *endorsements*. Endorsements restrict or expand coverage. Since policies are required to conform to differing state statutes, endorsements are sometimes included by one state but not another. Some endorsements are directed by the companies themselves and must be specifically excluded by a policyholder. For example, in some states companies add an endorsement covering credit card losses to their homeowners policies. You must specifically refuse the coverage if you do not want it or are covered by another policy.

And of course, you may specify endorsements to cover things not in the general form, or to exclude something like the credit card endorsement to save money. Endorsements enable you to fine-tune the policy's coverage as far as possible within the constraints allowed by your state's laws.

The Price Tag

An insurance premium is the bill for the coverage provided. There are various ways of paying your premiums. If you pay the premium in installments, the total paid is usually higher than if you pay in a single payment each anniversary. The administrative costs of handling multiple payments are higher and naturally that cost will be passed on to you. Typically, you are charged interest on the outstanding balance of your bill.

There are numerous payment options. In some policies, premium plans can be constructed so that premiums are small in earlier years and larger in later years. This applies primarily to life insurance. We will be covering some of these options in detail in Chapter 6.

If you cancel your coverage before the end of the policy's term, you may receive a refund. However, that is dependent on the company's short-rate cancellation table and refund policy. Normally, short-rate cancellations are heavily front-end weighted. This means that if you cancel early, you will not get a straight-line, prorata refund. If you have paid for your auto coverage for a full year and then cancel after six months, the short-rate cancellation cost may be as high as 75 percent or more of the premium paid. Instead of getting back 50 percent of the premium as you may have expected, you will usually get substantially less. This is why most reputable insurance agents want to know the expiration of your current coverage before writing the new policy.

The Marketplace

In exchange for a fee, insurance companies take the financial burden from your shoulders (underwriting) by pooling risk and paying for actual losses (claims) out of their reserves. Basically, you undertake a small but certain loss (the premium) to avoid the danger of a much larger potential loss (your house, your car, a lawsuit, etc.).

Insurance companies profit through underwriting and investing. If actual losses are below expected losses the company makes an underwriting profit That could mean either the company is very efficient, attracts good risks, is lucky, or is charging premiums that are too high.

An insurance company earns investment profit when its invested reserves (premiums put aside to cover potential losses) earn a return greater than its investment costs. This profit simply indicates the company is a good investment manager.

Types of Insurance Companies

There are five kinds of insurance companies. They are all regulated by the states in which they operate. They are:

1. *stock companies* which are owned by the stockholders;
2. *mutual companies* which are owned by the policyholders;
3. *health expense associations* which are founded by hospitals and doctors;
4. *Lloyd's of London* which is a group of many syndicates that provide coverage for unusual things such as horses' legs, singers' voices, very expensive jewelry, and the like;
5. *reciprocals* which involve business insurance and so won't be covered here.

Stock companies are owned by stockholders. Profits belong to stockholders and are paid in the form of dividends or retained earnings. Most property and casualty policies are written by stock companies. Stock companies offer two types of policies. A *participating* (par) policy returns a portion of the premium at the end of the policy period. Called a *dividend*, it is actually a refund of part of your premium, not a payment of earnings. Don't be fooled by the company's apparent largess in refunding part of your premium. They have been using your money and are merely refunding some of it. While it may make you feel good to see a dividend credit on your premium notice, you have not really earned anything or you would have to pay taxes on it. What you have done is give the insurance company an interest-free loan.

The other type of policy is called *nonparticipating* (nonpar). This type does not give you back anything on your anniversary date. However, it may be cheaper. And remember, the dividend of the participating policy is never guaranteed anyway.

Mutual companies are owned by their policyholders. The policyholder actually gets a piece of the pie when there is a profit. Most life and health policies are written by mutual companies. These profits are real, taxable dividends, unlike those distributed by stock companies to their participating policyholders. Theoretically at least, the greater the profits the larger the dividends.

There has been a long and inconclusive argument about whether stock or mutual companies offer the least expensive product. Those who argue that stock companies offer the best prices argue that stock companies are forced by the profit motive to be more efficient and offer products at the best rate. Mutual company proponents retort that since mutual companies do not have to pay dividends, they offer the lowest rates and pass on gains to policyholders during good times. As we said, the whole debate is inconclusive. You need to check with both stock and mutual companies to determine which offers the best policy for your situation at the lowest price.

Health expense associations are insurance organizations formed by hospitals and physicians' groups to provide medical services. Rather than paying the insureds, they make payments directly to doctors according to a specific fee structure. These groups make money by offering medical services at the lowest cost. That contrasts with corporate insurers who make money by selecting good risks.

Health expense associations offer two types of plans. *Closed-end* plans stipulate that all medical services must be provided only by member hospitals and physicians. *Open-end* plans allow members to get medical care from the doctor or hospital of their choice. Open-end plans are generally more expensive. Blue Cross and Blue Shield are the two largest health expense organizations.

Lloyd's of London is an insurance group made up of many subgroups or syndicates. Each syndicate is composed of 10 to 100 individuals who invest in insurance risks. Unlike other insurers that specialize in certain risks, Lloyd's gathers different types of risk exposures together in the same syndicate. In that way they balance certain risk exposures against the experiences of other risks. Lloyd's insures very large risks to which there may only be one or two exposures. You may have read about a professional football player acquiring a Lloyd's of London policy prior to practicing, if he is in contract negotiations. Virtually anything that is insurable can be done through Lloyd's. Lloyd's of London is licensed to sell its services in only a few states in the United States.

WRAPPING UP

Insurance is a way of protecting yourself from financial hardships that may result from calamities. By transferring your financial risk to an insurance company, you trade a certain loss (your premium) for the peace of mind of knowing you are protected from a major loss.

It is important that you know exactly what you want to insure. People have widely varying tolerances for loss. You need to take the time to prioritize your needs and to decide what you want to be protected against, how much you want to insure for, how long you want to insure for, and with whom you want to insure.

If you take the time to research the market and shop around, you will find that insurance is always a buyer's market. It is of little importance what type of insurance company you decide to do business with. You are interested in the coverage, the cost, and the service—not the organizational structure. Finding that right combination and staying with what is best for you requires periodic reviews of your coverages as well as the initial search process.

CHAPTER 3

COMPREHENSIVE LIABILITY AND AUTO INSURANCE

In order to better understand the underlying principles of insurance—the difference between protection afforded by insurance and that provided by building a nest egg—it is time to look into the details of the different types of insurance you may need. The best place to begin is with liability insurance.

You have no doubt read or heard about large legal settlements resulting from a wide range of lawsuits. There is no way to know in advance just how far-fetched some of these claims and awards can be. In one case, a woman who fell off a streetcar in San Francisco claimed that the fall caused her to become a nymphomaniac. She won a very large settlement! In another case, a jury awarded a woman $986,000 because she claimed to have lost her psychic powers after a CAT scan. Another person won a settlement for an injury to his back that he sustained while participating in a refrigerator-carrying footrace.

There are literally thousands of liability cases settled every year. While most make more sense than these examples, there are hundreds of fringe cases like these that ultimately cost thousands of dollars in legal fees even if the case is lost by the person filing the claim. In this chapter we cover general liability and automobile insurance. Unlike property insurance, such as homeowners, liability insurance pays money to others, not to you. However, your premiums cover the cost of services such as investigating and settling claims against you.

Automobile insurance is the most important type of liability coverage most people will have. Over two thirds of all civil liability lawsuits arise from auto accidents. Here we show you how to determine what kind and how much coverage you need.

LIABILITY AND YOU

Figuring out how much liability insurance you need is not quite as simple as totaling up your assets from your financial statements. There are many variables in making that determination that only you can know. For example, you will need to give some thought to your and your family's typical activities.

Do you play racquetball, basketball, baseball, or other sports and activities that involve other people? If so, your potential exposure increases. For example, a partner in a basketball game may claim that it was your fault (carelessness or negligence) that he fell and broke his wrist. The injury may have ended a promising career as a concert pianist. Since he may feel a deep resentment, he may decide to sue you for ruining his career and high-income potential. If he sues, it may mean a substantial expenditure on your part to defend the claim. And that large, out-of-pocket expense could occur whether or not his claim is justified.

Do you have pets? A dog may rush out of the house and bite a stranger passing by. Your cat may get into a neighbor's home and demolish a collection of rare antique glassware. Even when you walk your small dog on a leash, it may dart in front of an elderly pedestrian and cause an accident. What if your harmless parakeet took to making kamikaze attacks on visitors? Any of these circumstances can lead to expensive suits against you.

Do you or any family member own or drive a car, motorcycle, recreational vehicle (e.g., snowmobiles, ATV, boat), or even a bicycle? As we mentioned above, auto claims are the largest single source of liability suits. However, damage incurred by any vehicle driven or owned by you may subject you to substantial liability exposure. What type of property do you own? If your house has a swimming pool, basketball hoop, or some other attractive nuisance that may lure children (or carefree adults) into harmful situations, you have a higher risk than an apartment dweller.

Table 3-1 will give you a good idea of the types of policies you should consider. Fitting the right policy to your needs entails knowing your potential. Determining the correct amount of each coverage entails considering your financial state and certain subjective evaluations.

The most important of these subjective judgments is your financial position and visibility. You certainly should be familiar with your financial statements; but also consider how much of your real or perceived wealth is apparent to others because of your profession or the manner in which you live? Some professions are considered very high-income fields of endeavor. Are you high-profile yourself? If you are well-known, or perceived to be wealthy (the perception is more important than the reality!), your liability exposure is increased considerably.

This visibility factor is difficult to define. It comes down to clues such as the kind of car you drive, the size, location, and style of your home, your social circle, the kinds of vacations you take, and so forth. If you belong to an exclusive country club, you will appear far more affluent than someone who does his swimming and socializing at the YMCA. You are apt to get sued more readily and for much more.

TABLE 3–1
Policy Choices for Liability Insurance

You (or anyone under your care)	Policy Type	What's Covered
As someone who might make a mistake behind the wheel of a car	Family auto policy (separate limits) Special auto policy (single limit)	Bodily injury and property damage liability if your fault; liability of an uninsured or underinsured motorist if his fault; medical expenses regardless of who is at fault; physical damage coverage of your car regardless of who is at fault
	Package policy (single limit)	Same as above, plus home and personal property
As someone who might make a mistake behind the wheel of something other than a car	Leisure vehicle coverage	Same as auto, plus additional living expenses (if forced to live elsewhere while vehicle is being repaired); miscellaneous personal property in the leisure vehicle if it is your fault
As someone who might make a mistake anywhere else	Comprehensive (Section II) coverage of your homeowners policy Catastrophic liability policy (umbrella)	Bodily injury and property damage liability if your fault; medical expenses regardless of who is at fault

Four Types of Liability Exposure

Your liability exposure can and will vary greatly throughout your life. We have identified four general types of exposure that cover most cases. Each category has different insurance needs. In all likelihood, you will at some point fall into each of these categories as you progress through your life:

1. You are under 21 and covered by your parent's insurance.
2. You buy your first home. People begin to notice you.
3. Your net worth has climbed to between $25,000 and $100,000. People may begin to pay more attention because you are starting to appear more interesting.
4. Your net worth is over $100,000. Unless you have elected to drive an old clunker and dress in rags, you will be more financially visible. People may pay closer attention.

Maybe you don't fit exactly into any of these categories. But the important point is to recognize that when significant changes occur in your life, your insurance needs also change. Failure to adjust your coverage may mean you are paying too much for protection that you don't need, or you don't have enough protection.

Determining the Amount of Coverage You Need

You can buy liability insurance with virtually any limit you desire. The limits you select should be determined by the types of exposures you have. There are several methods for calculating how much liability insurance to buy. Below we discuss three of the more popular methods.

1. *Life value method.* With this approach you purchase enough comprehensive liability insurance to equal your present net worth (assets minus liabilities) plus the aggregate value of your future earnings. For example, if you expect to earn an average of $25,000 for the next 40 years ($25,000 × 40 = $1,000,000), and your present net worth is $100,000, you should buy $1,100,000. The idea behind this approach is the very logical point that you cannot be successfully sued for more than what you have and what you will earn.

2. *Net worth method.* This method assumes that future income will not be attached to fulfill a claim. Therefore, buy just enough to cover your present net worth. While this would be the least expensive approach, it also is based on the potentially very weak premise that courts will not assess future income. Courts certainly have, and there is no reason to expect a change in the near future.

3. *Jury awards method.* With this approach you try to insure sufficiently to cover awards being assessed by local courts. For example, if the largest award for a bodily injury case in your area is $1,000,000, then insure to that amount. The problem here of course, is that new, higher awards are always being made. Also there are many factors that influence an award. Things such as pain and suffering, amount of permanent disability, past and future income, past and future medical bills, family and dependents, and much more make it virtually impossible to compare even what appear to be similar injuries and awards.

We don't recommend that you spend inordinate time worrying about coming up with an exact figure for your liability coverage. Typically, $100,000 or more is included automatically with your homeowners policy. Increases in that amount are relatively inexpensive. Your agent should be able to give you a good ballpark figure.

GENERAL LIABILITY COVERAGE

General liability policies offer coverage for a variety of potential situations. A situation in which you have *liability* is one in which you are legally bound to pay another person for damages. This differs from property insurance in which the insurance company pays you, rather than another party for damages. Typically, you will get your general liability coverage bundled with your homeowners policy. All homeowner policies provide for liability coverage protecting the interests of any family member living at home, or anyone under 21 for whom a family member is responsible. These policies cover you for activities at home as well as away. For example, if you accidentally set your room on fire while traveling abroad, your homeowners policy will probably protect you if the hotel sues you for reimbursement.

General liability policies cover liability to others including damage to others' property. However, they normally do not cover slander, libel, or actions involving motor vehicles. You need to obtain an umbrella policy for the former and a specific auto liability policy for the latter.

Jacket Provisions

Jacket provisions stipulate that the insurance company will make payments for items such as expenses incurred investigating claims and defending your interests, court and bail bonds, and other reasonable expenses (including up to $50 a day for missed salary while attending legal hearings). Other jacket provisions include:

1. The insurance company reserves the right to inspect your property at any time.
2. You must notify the company in writing of any occurrence that has or may lead to a claim.

3. If two or more policies for the same coverage exist, each insurance company pays only its share of the total coverage.

Coverage Provisions

Comprehensive policies cover you and your family members for bodily injury and property damage from incidents that occur around the home to guests and others and from the acts of household members or pets. If you dump lasagna on a dinner guest's silk dress, your insurance will cover its replacement. Minimum liability coverage runs from $25,000 to $100,000. If you own property, you should consider carrying at least $300,000 to $500,000 coverage. Medical expenses, regardless of fault, are usually covered up to $500 (or higher if you want and pay for higher limits).

It is possible to buy supplementary coverage for minor damages up to $250 per accident regardless of fault. Even intentional damage caused by children under age 13 is covered by this supplementary coverage.

Liability policies distinctly exclude any damage for which you are responsible during business activities. This is true even when you are working part-time or moonlighting. This is frequently misunderstood and a cause of some chagrin, often after an accident has occurred.

For example, you may even find that if you get paid for babysitting in your home, you are not covered even though you would be covered if you were not getting paid. Attitudes and coverage vary with different companies. Be sure to ask your agent about it. You may need to get supplementary coverage. Most business activities must be covered in a separate comprehensive business policy. A good rule of thumb is to ask about anything which is not specifically covered in the jacket provisions of a policy. One question could save you a lot of money and anguish.

Umbrella Liability Policies

If you think you need additional protection, you will want to purchase an *umbrella policy*. Also often called *personal catastrophe insurance*, these policies extend and broaden your coverage. At one time this type of policy was only available to certain professionals subject to high-cost malpractice suits.

For example, if you are involved in political activities or do writing for organizations, you may want to have protection for slander or libel. That coverage is available through an umbrella policy.

Before you can purchase an umbrella policy though, you must maintain minimum limits of $50,000 to $100,000 on your homeowners comprehensive coverage and $250,000 to $300,000 on your auto insurance (limits vary from state to state).

Limits for umbrella policies run from $1,000,000 to $5,000,000. The annual cost can run as low as $150 in many states. That is a low price to pay for the added protection and peace of mind it affords.

If you own investment properties, it is a good idea to carry this coverage. The more property you own, the greater the possibility of someone getting hurt and suing you. It is also a good idea if you are in the limelight or have a tendency toward shoot-from-the-hip remarks about other people or organizations. As always, it depends on what you have to lose and how you feel about it.

THE NEED FOR AUTO INSURANCE

Auto insurance offers two major coverages: *liability* and *physical damage*. You are already familiar with liability coverage: it includes protection from claims resulting from bodily injury and property damage. This portion also includes uninsured motorist coverage (which we will explain later) and medical expenses for yourself and passengers in your car. See Table 3-2 for a summary of the types of auto insurance available and who is covered.

Physical damage coverage includes comprehensive and collision coverage. These coverages differ from liability coverage because they constitute payments to be made to you, rather than to other parties, for damages to your car.

Confusing this nice, clear-cut demarcation is *no-fault* insurance. Some 26 states have enacted no-fault laws. They vary widely though. No-fault insurance reimburses injured parties for their losses (medical expenses and loss of income) without regard to fault. It was designed to guarantee that injury victims would be compensated quickly no matter who is to blame. This approach theoretically would reduce the number of accident cases clogging the legal system.

Typically, each state's no-fault law has a set threshold of medical expenses. If accident victims' medical bills fall below that level, then they cannot pursue a liability claim through the courts. They are paid for their expenses and loss of wages by their own insurance company without regard to fault. Victims who have injuries requiring more than the threshold amount of medical bills would be allowed to sue to recover not only expenses but compensation for pain and suffering, inconvenience, and so forth.

Jacket and Coverage Provisions

Jacket provisions for auto insurance differ in one significant way from those of other liability policies: there is a *cancellation clause* which permits the company to cancel a *policy for any reason* during the first 60 days of the agree-

TABLE 3–2
Types of Auto Insurance and their Coverage

Type of Auto Insurance	Coverage Applying to:					
	Those in Your Car			Those in Car You Hit		
	Car and Property	Driver	Others in Car	Car and Property	Driver	Others in Car
Bodily injury liability		X*			X	X
Property damage liability				X		
Uninsured motorist		X	X			
Medical expense		X	X			
Comprehensive damage	X					
Collision damage	X					

*Only in states with no-fault insurance laws.

ment and with 30 days notice thereafter. Your policy can be canceled if you or any member of your household:

1. has a driver's license suspended;
2. becomes subject to heart attacks or epilepsy;
3. has three traffic violations within an 18-month period;
4. is convicted of a felony, criminal negligence with regard to the operation of a motor vehicle, or drunken driving.

Don't misunderstand though. While there is always the possibility that your insurance company can cancel your policy, typically they do not do so at the bat of an eye. Some prefer to simply raise their rates for you and seldom cancel.

Auto policies are similar to other comprehensive liability policies since they may be written to include coverage for bodily injury, property damage liability, and medical expense payments. Unlike other liability coverage though, auto policies offer physical damage coverage that acts in the same way as property insurance coverage.

You need to take extra care in selecting your auto policy to ensure that you get exactly the coverage you need. Some policies are written to provide only physical property damage coverage (often the lending institution for a new car will require this even if you pass on liability coverage). Other policies offer only liability coverage and afford no protection for damage to your own property.

Bodily Injury and Property Damage

Bodily injury and property damage liability coverage protects you and household members against claims while driving your car. Sometimes (check your policy) family members are covered while driving other people's cars and even rental cars.

Bodily injury limits are usually on a per person and per accident basis. You can choose from a range of bodily injury liability limits to suit your specific needs. A common one is $100,000/$300,000. This simply means that $300,000 is available from the company to pay for claims from an accident in which you are at fault. Only $100,000 of that amount though can be used for any one person.

Some companies offer single-limit coverage. This approach eliminates the $100,000 per person limit in the example above. The money is allocated to meet any injured party's expenses in whatever amounts are necessary within maximum coverage. This is obviously the preferred alternative if all other things are equal.

Most states have *financial responsibility laws* requiring a driver who has been in an accident that was his or her fault and that incurred bodily injury or property damage of more than a specified minimum amount (usually $50 to $250) to show proof of financial responsibility by posting a bond, depositing cash or securities with the state treasurer, or buying any auto liability insurance policy. Failure to comply subjects the driver to revocation of his or her driving privileges until financial responsibility can be proven.

Increasingly, states are requiring that all owners of motor vehicles show proof of insurance in order to register their autos. In June 1988, auto liability insurance coverage was mandatory in 39 states.

Property damage liability (damage to the other person's car and property) is usually written for $15,000, $20,000, or $25,000 per accident. This type of insurance is less complicated than bodily injury provisions since it is possible to accurately determine property damage. There is relatively little pain and suffering for property!

Uninsured Motorist Coverage

This provision supplies coverage in cases in which the driver at fault is not insured, or in hit-and-run cases. It primarily covers bodily injuries, but in some states this coverage is extended to property. While states set the minimum limits that are usually automatically included with your policy (unless you specifically request that it be excluded), it is possible to increase your limits.

What happens if you are involved in an accident in which your medical and other expenses are over $20,000 and the at-fault driver has only $10,000 coverage? You are out of luck unless (1) the other driver has other assets that can be attached, or (2) you bought *underinsured motorists coverage*. This relatively new addition to auto coverage also varies from state to state. It protects you for medical and disability coverage above and beyond the at-fault driver's coverage. In some states, though, it pays only if the limits in your policy exceed the liability coverage of the underinsured driver. In others, the only consideration is whether your damages exceed the other driver's liability limits.

Medical Expense Coverage

This provides payment for medical bills for any passenger in your car who sustains an injury regardless of who is at fault. Usually you are limited to expenses incurred within one year of the date of the accident. These expenses include medical supplies, X-rays, hospital expenses, dental care, ambulance costs, nursing care, and even funeral costs.

Coverage limits begin at $500. You can select whatever limit you feel is right. But remember, $500 doesn't go very far with medical costs as high as they are. Common limits run from $2,000 to $10,000. The rates for this additional coverage are quite low.

You don't have to crash into another car or wall to be eligible for medical expense payments. If you or a passenger catch a finger in a car door, it is still covered. You or family members would be covered if injured while riding in another person's car. And finally, your expenses would be covered if you were struck by another vehicle while you were a pedestrian.

Physical Property Damage Coverage

Physical damage coverage differs from liability coverage. It pays for the repair or replacement of your car, its equipment, and most things in it (stereos and CB radios are often excluded). There are two major coverage options: comprehensive and collision.

Comprehensive Coverage

This insures your car and its contents against loss from occurrences other than crashes. For example, it covers such things as theft, vandalism, malicious mischief, riot, civil commotion, and falling objects (trees, branches, birds, etc.). It also covers Mother Nature's perils such as earthquakes, windstorms, hail, water and flood damage, fire, and lightning.

The contents of the car must be owned by you or family members. If your neighbor left his stereo in your car overnight and it was stolen, your comprehensive coverage would not pay for it. You would have to turn to your property insurance to see what and how much is covered.

This provision also compensates you for renting a car if yours is stolen. This coverage is sold with a deductible. Changing the deductible amount has a substantial effect on the premium. A higher deductible will lower your premium.

Collision Coverage

When you buy that new car, your primary interest is usually ensuring that any damage to it can be fixed. If you are not familiar with liability, it is your only concern! That is where collision coverage comes into play. It pays for damage to your car from impact with another vehicle, an object, or the earth (a rollover) regardless of who is at fault.

Collision coverage is separate from comprehensive because the probability of an auto accident occurring is much greater than the incidents enumerated above.

Collision coverage makes up a substantial part of your premium. Since an insurance company will pay only for repairs up to the current book value of your car, and since many cars depreciate to about one-third of their selling value in five years, you may want to consider dropping your collision coverage and self-insuring if your car is five or more years old. This does not apply, of course, to classic cars which must have special coverage.

Fitting Coverage to Your Needs

You are the one who pays the premium, and what you pay for is what you get. Since virtually any coverage is possible (it is only a matter of money), it is important to relate coverage to your needs in order of priority. For instance, bodily injury coverage is the single most important element in your auto coverage because it shields you from the largest losses. With today's medical costs skyrocketing, it does not take much of an injury to incur huge medical bills. Property damage coverage rates closely behind, because one accident could cause the loss of that newly purchased car that can be ruinous to your net worth.

Unlike accidents around your home, the person injured while you are driving is likely to be a stranger who couldn't care less about any sad stories of yours. If you drive through the largest display window in the town square at high noon, that stranger may be a cold, anonymous organization that may hit you with a claim for all it can get.

Also, it would be wise to carry high property-damage limits. If you were to strike a single power pole that serviced three or four companies like the electric company, the telephone company, and cable television, the bill could easily exceed $10,000. These may not be the only claimants in an accident either. Often state highway department and municipal governments will join private businesses who own property in the path of your accident in filing claims against you. And remember, the owner of the other vehicle is also entitled to compensation. Your bill could mount to over $50,000 quickly.

Physical Property Damage Coverage

The amount of physical property damage coverage you carry should depend on the market value of your car. You can decrease the premiums by increasing your deductible as we have already discussed. This is the one area where you can reasonably self-insure, depending on your car's replacement value.

The way to determine whether you need collision coverage is to compare the out-of-pocket cost if your car were destroyed sans insurance with the cost of the premium. Using Table 3-3, "Market Value of John Doe's Car over the Last Four Years" and Table 3-4, "John Doe's Potential Loss and Insurance Outlays over the Next Four Years" will help you make calculations for your own car(s).

For this example, assume that John Doe's car is four years old. He originally purchased it for $10,000. Table 3-3 reflects the depreciation over the last four years. The replacement cost of his auto is $3,200 today. When you calculate the combined depreciation and accumulated premium, John would only get back a net of $82 in two years.

It obviously does not make sense to continue to pay this high annual premium. Of course, your loss experience and expectations will play a role. If you tend to total your car every year or so, you would want to keep the coverage

TABLE 3–3
Market Value of John Doe's Car over the Last Four Years

Age (years)	Depreciation Factor*	Dollar Depreciation (depreciation factor × original cost)	Market Value
New	0%	$ 0	$10,000
1	25	2,500	7,500
2	18	1,800	5,700
3	14	1,400	4,300
4	11	1,100	3,200

Journal of American Insurance, American Mutual Insurance Alliance.

(though we doubt the insurance company will continue to insure you for long). Remember, your insurance company will not pay more than the replacement cost of your vehicle. What is the depreciated value of your car? To get a quick idea, check the classified ads in your local newspaper, or check out the *Kelley Blue Book* prices at your library.

At this point, the insured should either determine what difference a higher deductible would make in his premium or should soon drop the coverage. Though, before dropping coverage altogether, be sure you have a ready cash reserve to replace your car if you do have an accident. It doesn't make much sense to pay as much in premiums over the next few years as your car itself is worth!

This procedure is more applicable for collision losses than comprehensive. You play a big role in your collision claims. By driving more carefully or less often you can minimize the risk of collisions. It is more difficult to control the acts of nature such as hail, windstorms, or earthquakes that comprehensive covers. Comprehensive coverage is often worthwhile to buy even when collision is not appropriate financially.

Medical Expense and Uninsured Motorist Coverage

Even if you already have adequate health and disability insurance, you can't be sure about the passengers in your car. It is wise to include a few thousand dollars of medical expense coverage with your policy. Some companies make it mandatory for at least $500 to $1,000. It is inexpensive.

You are also providing quick medical reimbursement for your passengers. They will not have to go through the aggravation of a lawsuit just to get bills paid quickly and without hassle.

TABLE 3-4
John Doe's Potential Loss and Insurance Outlays over the Next Four Years

Time	Market Value	Annual Premium*	Cumulative Premium plus $100 Deductible	Difference in Potential Loss and Accumulated Insurance Outlay
Today	$3,200	$406	$ 606	$2,594
One year from now	2,500	406	912	1,388
Two years from now	1,400	406	1,318	82
Three years from now	500	406	1,724	(1,224)
Four years from now	500	406	2,130	(1,630)

*Assumed to stay level to simplify the calculations. In reality, the premiums will rise each year as rates in general rise.

If your state has a generous no-fault law, this coverage is not as important as in states which are without no-fault or nonmandatory insurance. Since most uninsured motorist policies will not pay for property damage, if you have good medical coverage, this provision is of limited value.

Typically, the minimum coverage is $10,000 to $15,000 mandated by state law. In areas where there are a large number of uninsured drivers, the costs for increased limits may be quite high. Balance the need for coverage with your other coverage, especially your health insurance.

No-Fault Insurance: Principles and Problems

No-fault insurance originated as an effort to avoid long and costly court battles that resulted in verdicts that were often too small or overly generous with little rhyme or reason. The subjective element of the jurors' emotions made it very difficult to plan on any continuity. The argument behind no-fault emphasized that by eliminating huge attorney's fees, which range from one third to one half of the total damage settlements, insurance costs would be lowered and the savings would be passed on to policyholders.

No-fault insurance reimburses injured parties for their economic losses from auto accidents (medical expenses and loss of income) without regard to fault. You receive payments from your own insurance company without having to go through an adversarial settlement process. Claims for things like pain and suffering are available only to people who meet certain threshold limits such as permanent injury or a minimum level of expenses incurred. To date, the argument over the virtues of no-fault is far from settled. However, there is little doubt that it is spreading as one answer to rising rates. Successful no-fault laws have been in operation in Saskatchewan, Canada since 1946 and Puerto Rico since 1969. Since 1971 when Massachusetts was the first state to adopt no-fault, a number of other states have followed. However, the debate still rages over rising rates. Insurance companies argue that their costs have not come down because these no-fault laws are hybrids that still keep the tort liability (determining who is at fault and how much they must pay) system for the many exceptions to the rule.

But if you think insurance policy options are confusing, wait until you see the very wide variances that exist from state to state over no-fault laws. If you live in a state that now has these laws, you should ask your insurance agent how your policy deals with the following issues:

1. Amount paid for medical or death expenses.
2. Amount paid for loss of income to insured breadwinners.
3. Amount paid to replace services ordinarily performed by a nonincome-producing homemaker now injured.
4. Conditions allowing the right to sue.

5. Survivor benefits, if any.
6. Property damage coverage, if any.

The law varies so much from state to state on just these issues that we cannot give you an accurate sketch of typical coverage.

INSURANCE RATES: UPS, DOWNS, AND WAYS AROUND

Insurance rates have been moving sharply higher due to inflation and skyrocketing medical costs. There is no easy solution to the problem. Auto insurance rates have risen at a steady 9 percent per year since 1980. The rising rates have triggered angry responses by both consumers and regulators. In 1988 California voters were faced with five different proposals that were supposed to result in lower insurance costs. Other states, including Florida and Massachusetts, were contemplating major changes to their insurance systems.

Rate-making is based on past experience of drivers in a given area and the total amount of claims paid out by insurance companies. Rating systems vary between companies. In fact, many companies' rates vary by areas. For example, a *rating territory* may be a city, a section of city, a suburb, or a rural area. Preferred risks may pay less than the standard rate, while those who are accident prone may pay more.

Some of the other important variables that determine your insurance costs include the type of car you drive, who drives it, why, how far, how often it is driven, and last but certainly not least, the insurance company you choose.

Safe driver plans, like most other rating systems vary from company to company. Generally, points are assigned for each traffic violation or accident that is your fault. The number of points you accumulate (or don't) determines a premium increase or decrease. It shows how, despite all the howls, you can control your insurance premiums in some measure.

Points range from zero if your auto is damaged by a hit-and-run driver or you pay for a claim, to three points for drunk driving and other serious charges involving recklessness.

Age and Rates

It is a fact that people under 25 years old make up more than one fifth of the nation's drivers. Yet they account for more than one third of all people involved in accidents. Drinking plays a role in about half the cases.

It is because of this poor group record that your premiums soar when your children turn 16 and can't wait to drive the family car. However, you will find that it is far cheaper in most cases to cover your dependent under your policy than to buy a separate one. There are numerous discounts available for even young drivers. For example, most companies have a good student program that affords discounts if your driving age children maintain a B grade average. There are also discounts offered for completing an approved driver's education course and/or going to school 100 or more miles from home.

The magic number at which a driver is no longer considered youthful is 25 for women and 30 for men. At that age, depending on the driver's experience, premium rates are usually reduced substantially. And often, 40 years later when a person turns 65 and has maintained a good driving record, a premium discount is offered. Age has its merits. And marriage will largely cancel out the premium that youth has to pay.

Other Variables

If you drive a car for pleasure only (not even to and from work) and for less than 6,500 miles per year, you will probably qualify for a lower rate.

Insurance companies take into consideration the size and type of your car. These rate differences are based on insurance company records of claims for each type of car. A car with a good track record can earn you a 30 percent discount. Choose one with a poor record and you could pay a 10 to 30 percent surcharge! If saving money is your goal, high-performance and sports cars are not the right choice. Stay with station wagons and four-door sedans.

Your insurance agent should be able to provide you with an up-to-date list of cars that trigger both discounts and surcharges. If you want to delve further into this issue, write the Institute for Highway Safety, Publications Department, Watergate 600, Suite 300, Washington, DC 20037 for its report on the claims experience of over 170 makes and models.

If you do not use your car for business purposes, you will be able to save. If you can cut your weekly commuting distance to less than 30 miles round-trip you can cut as much as 10 to 30 percent from your total premium.

In recent years some companies have been offering discounts for non-smokers and members of certain professions such as doctors or lawyers. Other discounts have been offered for safety items such as automatic seat belts and air bags. And remember, it is usually cheaper to insure all your cars through one company since they usually offer a multicar discount. If you have your home-owners insurance with the same company as your auto policy, you may qualify for a multipolicy discount.

Where you drive is critical. All other things being equal, a person who drives in New York City will pay far more than someone driving in rural New York.

Check Up on Yourself

Take advantage of every discount you can. Check with your agent about every item that might apply to you.

☐ Student away at school   ☐ Car pool
☐ Senior citizen   ☐ Antitheft devices
☐ Honor student   ☐ Woman, age 30-64, only driver
☐ Nonsmoker or nondrinker   ☐ Pleasure driving only
☐ Driver's training   ☐ Farmer or clergyman

Assigned Risk Plans

What used to be called *assigned risk plans* are now a state-regulated assigned risk pool of drivers known as a *shared market*. When drivers with poor records are unable to secure coverage from companies, they are assigned by the state to an insurance company that must cover them for the state-mandated liability limits for three years.

Every insurance company must accept a percentage of these drivers. Neither the driver nor the company has any choice about who is assigned to whom. You could end up assigned to a company that previously refused to cover you. But you can be assured that it will charge you a higher premium than it would have if it had accepted you voluntarily. If you receive a traffic citation while under this coverage, there will be a steep surcharge on your premium.

In most cases, there is no question about your being able to find insurance coverage one way or another. Your coverage may be limited though. If you have to go the assigned pool route, keep your performance clean for three years, the chances are that you will have no problem being accepted on a regular basis by the same or another insurance company after that time.

Shopping Around

A particular company's rates will vary depending on which variables it holds near and dear, its loss experience, and its market. For example, one company that offers the lowest rates for a married couple in their 40s with no driving-age children, may have the highest rates when you buy another kind of car or get a traffic ticket. It pays to shop around. Rates may be a lot higher or lower between companies.

The company that considers you an excellent risk today because you are over 25, married, and have no driving-age children may consider you tarnished when your youngster reaches driving age. It is a good idea to shop around whenever you renew your insurance policy. For this reason, we have provided you with Action Paper No. 1, "Shopping for Auto Insurance" to facilitate your comparison shopping. The action paper is located at the back of the book. It is self-explanatory. Just make a few phone calls and fill in the blanks. There is no easier way to make a comparison. It is right in front of you in black and white.

AFTER AN AUTO ACCIDENT

When you have been in an accident and are not seriously hurt, it is important to accomplish a number of things before leaving the scene:

1. Get help for any injured person as quickly as possible.
2. Protect yourself and your car from any further damage by setting up flares, turning on your car's emergency flashers, or taking some other appropriate cautionary action.
3. Call the police.
4. Find out how you can get a copy of the completed police report.
5. In *all* cases, get the full name of the other driver(s), their complete street and mailing addresses, drivers license number, and the name of their insurance company and agent.
6. Get the full names and addresses of any witnesses if possible.
7. As soon as practical, write a description of the accident. It is always easier to remember details while it is still fresh in your memory.
8. Take photos if possible, or make a sketch of the accident scene.
9. Most important, notify your insurance company as soon as possible. Do it the same day if you can. Some companies require that all accidents be reported to them within 48 hours for them to be covered.

Making a Claim

When you have an accident and it is not your fault, you will most likely file a claim with the erring party's insurance company. There are a number of important things you should know about the procedure that a company will follow and how you should respond to reach a suitable settlement.

The claims adjuster is the official link between you and the other driver's insurance company. The adjuster's job is threefold:

1. Determine what kind of person you are, the extent of your injury, your desire to get well, and the extent of damage to your vehicle.

2. Estimate the amount of money that the insurance company will probably have to pay to come to a satisfactory settlement. This estimate is the *reserve* set aside by the insurance company to meet its potential future obligations.
3. Settle the claim as quickly as possible by delivering a check to you.

In order to do their job, adjusters will ask you a number of questions about how the accident happened, who was at fault, what your medical condition is, and things of that nature. They will also ask a number of questions about you such as your background, your job, your income, and your medical history. In order to settle an injury claim they will ask for copies of a doctor's report and medical bills.

It is alright to speak with an adjuster but you should be very cautious about what you say. Don't answer questions about your medical background. That is for doctors to discuss, not laymen. It is generally best to be pleasant but uninformative. Remember, the adjuster is working for the other driver and would like to find evidence that fault lies with you rather than with their insured.

Once the necessary information has been gathered, the adjuster will estimate the value of the claim. This is simply what the adjuster feels, based on the investigation, your claim is worth. It is certainly not carved in stone! They will try to settle the claim as soon as possible. It is in the interest of the insurance company to close claims as quickly as possible to minimize their expenses.

Different companies handle claims differently. Some companies will pay your expenses as you go along rather than making you pay all your expenses up front, then working out a settlement. Other companies prefer to work with a single lump-sum payment and release it when you are ready (though they will often try to convince you that you are ready sooner than you think). However, no claim is complete until you have signed a release. Contrary to popular belief, mere acceptance of a check does not release the company from any future claims. Some insurance companies do include a release from on the back of their checks. If you are not satisfied that your claim is complete, do not endorse the check. Your right to future claim is not ended until you sign a release leaving open the chance that any further expenses incurred as a direct result of the accident will be paid.

Sizing Up the Damages

After visiting with you and the client of the company the adjuster represents, investigating the scene of the accident, talking with witnesses, reading the police report, and checking out the physical evidence of the cars and the scene of the accident, the adjuster will value the case based on experience and company policy. He or she will take into consideration your total medical expenses (incurred and estimated future), the amount of income loss due to your impaired condition, and any other expenses you or your family incurred such as babysitting, housecleaning, clothes, and personal property damage or loss.

There are many different ways to value claims. A common approach is to use a multiplier (often three) to figure pain and suffering. For example, if the total of the items mentioned above is $3,000, the pain and suffering amount may be $9,000 (3 × $3,000). The adjuster would advise the company that the claim is worth $12,000 ($3,000 expenses plus $9,000 pain and suffering). The company sets aside a reserve of that amount.

Obviously, an insurance company will want to settle claims as quickly as possible. However, remember the statute of limitations is one or two years in most states. This means you have that long after an accident to file a lawsuit protecting your rights. If there is a chance you will have continuing medical problems, don't sign a release until you have gotten your doctor's okay.

It is possible to structure your settlement in a number of ways. Often you may need money before all your medical bills are in. Most insurance companies are flexible in working out settlements. It is to their advantage to deal directly because they can save the huge legal fees of an attorney.

However, keep in mind that there are unscrupulous claims adjusters just as there are people of questionable ethics in all professions. If you suspect something, or if the adjuster does not follow through with a promise, do not hesitate to go to your state's insurance commissioner, or retain an attorney if you have any doubts.

If your injury is a serious and expensive one, it may be in your interest to hire an attorney. That will depend on your relationship with the insurance company. Their policies and adjusters vary widely. Don't prejudge their claims policy any more than you would their insurance policies without first checking it out yourself.

Often the threat of an attorney will bring stalled negotiations to an agreement. Insurance companies know that an attorney will mean delays and more expenses over the long term.

WRAPPING UP

By learning and applying what you have assimilated about comprehensive liability and auto insurance, you have put money in the bank. You now know that liability policies cover all liability exposure other than that concerning the operation of motor vehicles and that involving slander and libel. You also know how inexpensive such liability policies can be when matched against what you stand to lose in a vulnerable position.

Check Up on Yourself

☐ Have adequate bodily injury coverage

☐ Have adequate property damage coverage

☐ Have adequate medical expense coverage

☐ Have adequate comprehensive coverage

☐ Have underinsured motorist protection

☐ Have uninsured motorist protection

☐ Decide to keep or cancel collision

☐ Check rates yearly

☐ Check jacket provisions

☐ Understand no-fault insurance

☐ Understand point system

☐ Maintain accident expense record

☐ Need bicycle or moped insurance

☐ Need umbrella policy

☐ Keep notebook in car

☐ Ask agent questions

Now you understand the importance of auto liability protection. It represents your greatest liability exposure. You understand the difference between liability and collision coverage. Whether or not to buy collision coverage depends on the value of your car. You know that it is important and can make a big difference in premium dollars to shop around for the best rates on all types of insurance policies.

And finally, you will no longer be intimidated by how to go about handling a claim, if you are unfortunate enough to have the experience. Congratulations! At this point you already know far more than the average person about the frightening world of liability insurance.

CHAPTER 4

PROPERTY INSURANCE

Take a quick look around your home. What would happen if you lost everything in a fire? Do you have sufficient savings to replace everything without causing a sharp change in your lifestyle? Consider just the items you are financing. If your television were stolen or your washer and dryer destroyed by fire, do you have sufficient reserves to not only buy replacements but to pay off the balance of the loans on them?

Many people never realize just how much they possess until or unless they experience a loss. And even if they have some type of insurance, those who just bought a standard package are often dissatisfied with their settlement. As we have been stressing, it is critical to know and plan your insurance needs around your particular circumstances. You don't want to be one of those people who is surprised to find out how much your possessions are really worth only after they have been lost!

Once you understand the threat that legal liability can pose to your financial well-being, you realize that comprehensive liability and auto insurance play a crucial part in your financial planning. Properly selected property insurance can play an equally important role in relieving your uneasiness over the threat of loss, through fire or theft, of the property you use and rely on daily.

Your possessions probably represent your largest investment. Most investors first accumulate personal possessions, then build their investment portfolios. What you own is part of your identity. Your possessions may tell more about you than you imagine. Remember, in the last chapter we told you that one of the principal considerations in determining how much liability insurance you need is your financial visibility.

In this chapter we concentrate on the types of property you can and should insure. We show you how to inventory and evaluate the things you value. We explain the most important considerations of the many types of policies that are available. And last but surely not least, we discuss premiums and ways you can save money while getting the protection you need.

40

WHAT PROPERTY CAN BE INSURED?

If you are a homeowner, your first thought when someone mentions property is probably your home. But that may not even be your largest investment when you consider the value of all your other assets. For insurance purposes, the term *property* refers to two distinct categories: *personal property* (your belongings: books, TV, stereo, appliances, furniture, and so on) and *real property* (physical structures, most commonly a house). Land is real property too, but is not insurable because it presumably cannot be destroyed.

You can insure anything that belongs to you (except land as we mentioned) that has a determinable value and would cause a monetary loss if destroyed, damaged, or stolen. That can include structures attached to your house (like your garage); unattached structures (like a toolshed or greenhouse); and the trees, plants, and shrubs around your house.

It can also include your personal property, either on the premises or away from home (like your children's possessions when away at college). It can even include other people's property while it's on your premises. Property insurance can provide additional living expenses if a disaster like a fire forces you to move elsewhere for awhile.

The Role of Property Insurance

Insurance plays a bigger part in the protection of the things you own than anything else. For this reason it deserves your careful attention. A few minutes spent carefully determining the appropriate insurance coverage will save you both money now and grief later if the worst occurs. You know the old saying: "If it weren't for bad luck, I wouldn't have any luck at all."

Insurance companies usually reserve the right to refuse coverage on property with unusually high risk, such as one that doesn't meet minimum fire safety standards due to outdated wiring or one that is in violation of building or safety codes. In certain locations, such as densely populated areas with primarily wood construction, significantly higher insurance rates reflect the higher risk of casualties like fire.

Vacant buildings pose special problems. They are more accessible to vandals. Companies usually require that they be boarded up to be insurable.

Insurance can't cover all losses such as those for inflation or poor investment selection. And insurance companies seldom cover losses due to floods or mudslides. This can be confusing, but it makes sense when you understand that catastrophes such as floods and mudslides don't accommodate the risk-sharing principle that is the basis for insurance. In Chapter 2 we quoted the 1825 English explanation of the underlying principles of insurance:

> Whenever there is a contingency, the cheapest way of providing against it is by uniting with others, so that each man may subject himself to a small deprivation, in order that no man may be subjected to a great loss.

Property owners in areas where flooding or mudslides never occur (e.g., flat, near-desert land in the Southwest, much of the Midwest, and elsewhere) have no need for such coverage. Therefore, the risk cannot be spread equally among enough people to make it economical. Those who have no risk have no incentive to join with the smaller number who are at risk.

That is why it is not economical from an insurance company's standpoint to offer particular catastrophe insurance only to those most likely to be affected by flooding or mudslides. The same is true for earthquakes. However, as we explain later, all three risks *can* be insured against.

Market Value versus Replacement Cost

Before you take inventory of your personal effects there is one other important concept that you should understand: the difference between *market value* and *replacement cost*. In Chapter 3 you learned the importance of keeping track of your car's value relative to your collision coverage premium, since your insurance company will not pay you any more than the market value (or purchase price minus depreciation) if your car is damaged in an accident.

The market value of an item is simply the dollar value that you could receive if you sold the item. It is what similar items are selling for at the time. In the last chapter we mentioned that one good way to determine how much your insurance company would pay you if your car were totaled was to see what price comparable makes were selling for in the classified section of the local newspaper. That price is the market value. It reflects not only depreciation (decrease in value) or appreciation (increase in value) of that item but also the emotions of the buyer.

When you speak of most personal property, you don't tend to think of appreciation, but it does happen. For example, those antiques your mother has been collecting over the years may very well be appreciating. That first edition book you bought, that old presidential campaign button you find in a drawer, your old comic collection may all have appreciated substantially. But that value is often largely dependent on your finding the right buyer. Memorabilia collectors tend to be emotionally involved in their specialties rather than cold, calculating investors. Their emotions contribute mightily to the ultimate sale prices of those items.

On the other hand, *replacement cost* is virtually emotion free. It is simply the current price to buy a substantially equivalent replacement for the item that is lost. In the case of a house, replacement cost is the building contractor's estimate. As you can see, the type of coverage you have—market value (or as it is often called in insurance policies *actual cash value*) or replacement cost—can make a big difference in what you receive if a loss occurs.

If much of your personal property (such as furniture, clothing, appliances, etc.) is three, four, or five years old, you will receive a relatively small amount once the insurance adjuster subtracts depreciation from their purchase price. Historically, most property insurance has been based on coverage for market value. However, in recent years, many companies have begun to offer replacement cost coverage for an additional 5 percent to 15 percent premium.

If you have replacement cost coverage, you can ignore depreciation. Most policies with a replacement cost endorsement (endorsements are provisions that add nonstandard coverages to a policy) stipulate that if an insured item that is destroyed or stolen is not replaced, it is then valued at market value. This is so there is much less incentive for insured items being destroyed, or stolen in order to raise money. Providing a ready market for your belongings in case of monetary problems is not one of the roles of insurance!

DETERMINING WHAT YOU OWN AND ITS VALUE

When you buy a standard homeowners or renters insurance policy, many of your personal belongings are covered at home or away from home, as we mentioned. The catch is that they are insured for only their market value, which is only a fraction of their replacement value (you usually have to pay extra to get replacement cost coverage). Typically, your personal property coverage limit is 50 percent of the amount of coverage on your home's structure. If your personal belongings are wiped out by fire or theft, you would wind up with much less than their value to you personally.

Each insurance company also sets maximum limits on certain categories of belongings you wish to insure. For example, jewelry, furs, and manuscripts are typically limited to $1,000. Currency loss is limited to $200. Silverware or goldware may have an upper limit of $2,500 per loss. Watercraft, including trailers, is limited to $1,000. Protection for unauthorized charges in case your credit cards are stolen typically pays up to $500. Think about it. If just one item is worth that much or more and you lose everything, you will get only the specified limit amount.

That is why you may want to consider a Personal Articles Floater if these preset limits provide inadequate coverage. A Personal Articles Floater enables you to customize your coverage to fit your particular needs. We discuss floaters in more detail at the end of this chapter under "Finding the Right Type of Insurance Coverage."

Taking a Personal Property Inventory

What if a fire destroyed only two rooms in your home? Would you be able to list all the items that were lost in just these rooms? If your loss appears particularly high—say you lost a mink coat or other high priced item—how could you document that fact to your insurance company? A room-by-room inventory is valuable not only so you know what is lost, but to substantiate a claim to your insurance company.

A personal property inventory should be as easy to update as it is to acquire personal property. An inventory won't make your insurance any cheaper, but it will give you a solid idea of the overall worth of your belongings and how evenly you have distributed valuable items around your home. It should also set off warning signals when you are underinsured. And as we noted above, it can prove invaluable for documenting a loss claim.

Making a room-by-room inventory is tedious, but it is far easier than trying to do it after a burglary or fire. The sooner the better. Your insurance agent can provide you with appropriate forms. We have included Action Paper No. 2, "Your Personal Property Inventory" at the end of this book to help get you started.

We've completed a sample inventory form, Figure 4-1, to help you complete your own form. As we mentioned above, some insurance companies allow you to purchase replacement cost coverage (called a personal property replacement cost endorsement) for an additional premium of 5 percent to 15 percent. If this option is available, you can save some time with your own inventory since you won't have to worry about figuring depreciation. While you won't then have to complete items 4, 5, and 7, you still need to complete the inventory of your personal property. Complete an inventory for each room in your home.

Even though you have completed an inventory you should take additional steps to document your list. For example, take pictures of the interior of your home. If possible, use a video camera to better demonstrate what and where your furnishings are and the quantity of property in each room. In most large cities there are companies that will provide this video inventory for a fee. Or you may want to rent a video camera on your own.

This not a frivolous or work-making suggestion. It is simply a very useful precaution. Remember, the more preparation you do in advance, the smoother things will go if you do have a loss and need to make a claim. Keep your pictures and/or videotape and a copy of your personal property inventory in your safety deposit box or somewhere other than in your home. They will do you very little good if they are also lost in a fire!

FIGURE 4–1
Sample Action Paper No. 2,
Your Personal Property Inventory

Action Paper No. 2

Your Personal Property Inventory

Article Category	1 Number of Articles	2 Total Original Cost	3 Average Age (years)	4 Annual Depreciation	5 Total Depreciation	6 Today's Cost	7 Accumulated Dollar Depreciation	8 Market Value
Wall-to-wall Carpet	1 (15'x48')	$810	4	20%	80%	$1,013	$810	$203
African Area Rug	1 (10'x12')	$800	2	10%	20%	$950	$190	$760
Antique Chairs	4	N.A.	100	N.A.	N.A.	$400*	N.A.	$400
Sofa (11 foot)	1	$800	10	10%	100%	$1,400	$1,400	-0-*
Loveseat	1	$450	6	10%	60%	$550	$330	$220
Wall Cabinet Unit	1 (8'x8')	$900(sale)	8	7%	56%	$1,000	$560	$440
Coffee Table	1 (6'oval)	$400	10	***		$800	$80	$720
Piano (upright)	1	$400	20	7%	100%	$900	$900	-0-*
Drapes	4	$200	8	10%	80%	$300	$240	60
Venetian Blinds	4	$200(sale)	2	7%	14%	$240	$34	$206
Books (fiction)	50	$250	4	**		$250		$150
Antique mirror	1	N.A.	100	N.A.	N.A.	$150*	N.A.	$150
Lamps (electric)	5	$350	6	7%	42%	$385	$162	$223
Gas Lanterns	2	$100	4	7%	28%	$110	$31	$79
End Tables	4	$200(sale)	6	7%	32%	$280	$90	$190
Ship Models	2	N.A.	8	N.A.	N.A.	$500*	N.A.	$500
Stoneware Planters	2	$50	3	***		$55		$50
Mantle Clock	1	N.A.	100	N.A.	N.A.	$150*		$150
Oil Painting	1	$300	2	N.A.	N.A.	$350*	N.A.	$350
Picture Frames	8	$320	4	5%	20%	$400	$80	$320
Bronze Bust	1	$100	50	N.A.	N.A.	$350*	N.A.	?*
Brass Candle Sticks	2	$25	3	7%	21%	$40	8	$32
TOTAL	**88**	**$6,655**				**$10,573**		**$5,203**

* appraised value
** use 60% of replacement cost
*** use 90% of replacement cost

* may have some value (indeterminate)
N.A. - not applicable

Room: Living Room

Valuing Your Home

We have already discussed the difference between market value and replacement cost of property, but this difference is worth going into just a bit more because of the vital difference it makes in how you value your home for insurance purposes. Most insurance companies require policyholders to insure their homes and detached buildings, such as a garage, for replacement cost. But it is your responsibility as the homeowner to be sure these costs are up to date on your coverage. Every time you renew your policy (usually annually), it is critical that you check with a local contractor to ensure that you have insured for the proper amount. Construction costs rarely go down. As you will see in our discussion below of the coinsurance clause, you don't want to make a mistake here because it can make a big difference even if only part of your home is destroyed in some calamity.

To compute replacement costs, simply multiply the total square footage of your dwelling by the current construction cost per square foot. For example, assume your house is 2,000 square feet of standard frame construction (excluding garage). If the average construction cost in your neighborhood is $60 per square foot, the current replacement cost would be $120,000. If your home is specially situated and reconstruction would require unusual handling or equipment, then you will need to factor in additional costs. For a more reliable estimate, call a local contractor and ask the figure per square foot he or she would use to rebuild your home. You may even want to hire an appraiser to assure yourself of the most accurate figures.

The Coinsurance Clause

Many of the horror stories you hear about insurance companies' use of fine print to get out of making a fair settlement arise from misunderstanding the coinsurance clause. Understanding the coinsurance clause can mean a difference of thousands of dollars if you have damage to your property. It is not a clause to be scanned lightly!

The coinsurance clause states that the insurance company will pay for a covered loss in its entirety up to policy limits *only if your coverage limits are at least equal to 80 percent of the replacement cost of the home covered.* But if the coverage you are carrying on your home is less than 80 percent of the replacement cost, you will be penalized according to a formula spelled out in the policy such that you will be entitled to less than full replacement cost.

For example, if a fire should destroy your kitchen and you do not have coverage limits of at least 80 percent of the replacement value of your home, you will receive less than the full replacement value as determined by a dividing your actual coverage by 80 percent. It works this way: if the replacement cost for your kitchen is $15,000, and the replacement cost of your home is

$100,000, you will be reimbursed the full $15,000 only if you have at least $80,000 replacement cost coverage on your home. If you have only $70,000 coverage on your home, the amount you are entitled to receive is figured by dividing your actual coverage by 80 percent (70 ÷ 80 = 87.5 percent). You would get only $13,125. However, if the loss is equal to or exceeds 80 percent of the structure's replacement cost, the company will pay 100 percent up to the policy limits.

You may wonder what the connection is between the replacement value of your home and the replacement value of only one room if your coverage limits are sufficient to cover at least the damage to that room. The logic on the part of insurance companies is simple. Through the coinsurance clause, the insurance company guarantees that if it is going to provide maximum coverage, its policyholders will not benefit from underinsuring.

Remember, the insurance company makes money from the premiums it collects. If you try to save a few dollars in premiums by cutting your policy limits to the bone, it can cost you dearly if you have a loss that is less than policy limits. Therefore you have a strong incentive to be sure you are fully covered. This is yet another reason to be sure at renewal time that your coverage is adequate.

This often misunderstood but important concept bears repeating: according to the coinsurance clause, in order to collect the entire replacement cost for *any* damage to your house, even if only one door was destroyed, you still must have coverage on the *entire* house equal to at least 80 percent of its full replacement value. If you do not, you will not receive full replacement value from the insurance company for your loss.

The coinsurance clause comes into effect only when both the amount of insurance carried and the amount of the loss fall below 80 percent of the replacement cost.

Replacement and Inflation Cost Coverage

Many insurance companies now offer a *replacement cost endorsement* that shifts the responsibility for keeping replacement cost coverage up to 80 percent to the insurance company. With this, the company guarantees that it will replace your home even if it costs more than the policy stipulates it is insured for. Of course, if you purchase this option, the insurance company will insure you to the maximum. For instance, in our example above, even if you had requested only the $70,000 coverage, your insurance company would have required the $100,000 it would take to replace your home if you elected the replacement cost endorsement.

Naturally this alternative costs more. In some areas replacement cost coverage for structures is only 10 percent to 15 percent more, much like the increase for similar coverage on personal property. However, prices vary widely among companies and different geographic areas. In some cases the increase for this coverage can run as much as 300 percent over the price for basic coverage. In the latter case, it may be more prudent to stick with standard coverage and be sure that you keep the limits up to date yourself.

And remember, even though your insurance company is on the hook for a minimum of 80 percent of the replacement value of your home, if a loss occurs, the company doesn't have to cover the remaining 20 percent if costs have risen in the interim above the initial valuation. In other words, you can't simply assume that the insurance company will not undervalue the replacement cost of your property and leave you holding the bag for 20 percent. On a home, that 20 percent can be a lot of money. Check the numbers on your property insurance coverage regularly!

In the late 1970s inflation was a major concern in the economy. Since then many companies offer *inflation guard policies*. These policies typically adjust policy limits upward in line with some index, such as the consumer price index (CPI) or a nationwide construction index. Others simply adjust limits up 8 to 10 percent annually. However, regardless of what the adjustment does, this endorsement is not a substitute for either getting replacement cost coverage or calculating the appropriate limits yourself. Costs vary widely around the country. Historically, construction costs have risen at twice the level of the CPI. An inflation cost endorsement may create a false sense of security.

Improvements and Remodeling

Simply protecting the bank that holds your mortgage does not make good insurance sense. If you have made any significant improvements in your property, you should be sure to buy sufficient insurance to cover them.

One way to get full coverage is to buy a *full measure plus* endorsement. This provides that the amount of coverage on a dwelling, detached buildings, unscheduled personal property (personal property not specifically delineated in a policy floater), and additional living expenses shall apply as a *blanket* limit of liability for all the property mentioned, regardless of individual limits.

In other words, if your garage is accidentally set afire and destroyed, the insurance company will pay whatever it costs to replace it up to the full limits of your entire property policy. With this coverage the separate limits for each particular, such as personal property or detached structure, do not apply. All coverage limits are the same as the blanket.

FINDING THE RIGHT TYPE OF INSURANCE COVERAGE

By this time you have decided what property you want protected. Now you need to decide what perils to insure against. You know already that most insurance companies will not pay if you have intentionally done something destructive to your property. If you get mad and take an ax to your computer (they can get frustrating!) it won't be covered. Destruction caused by riots or civil disobedience is usually covered, but most companies won't pick up the tab if there is damage caused by a war.

There are four groups of policies that cover your home, your personal property, or both:

1. *Standard fire policies* cover your home and other physical structures against damage from fire. However, these policies cover only that one threat.

2. *Dwelling building and contents policies* cover all physical damage to a dwelling plus damage done by a burglar. However, these policies do not provide coverage for personal property that is stolen from your home.

3. *Renters and homeowners policies* are the most popular. They are designed to meet your needs as a renter or homeowner. Among these, *package policies* do the best job of covering everything, including auto insurance, all in one policy.

4. *Floaters* cover personal property wherever it goes in the world. They are designed to provide coverage for highly valued items such as furs, jewelry, paintings, antiques, elaborate computer systems, and other expensive possessions.

Property insurance policy choices are outlined in Table 4-1. Action Paper No. 3, "Shopping for Property Insurance" is provided at the end of this book to help you summarize your property needs and wants.

Homeowners Policies

Homeowners and renters policies are by far the most common property insurance policies written for individual consumers. They are package policies. That simply means they include different types of insurance—specifically, liability and personal and real property coverage in one policy. These policies cover your dwelling, any detached structures, unscheduled personal property, trees, plants, and additional living and medical expenses due to loss. They cover the cost of removing debris caused by damage. They also include up to $500 for fire department services.

Coverage is provided for personal property up to 10 percent of the total insured value of your personal property while in transit. Your personal property is covered to the full policy limits for up to 30 days in your new location. You must report your change of address to your insurance company within 30 days to continue coverage.

It is important to know the limits that are imposed on coverage for some stolen valuables such as currency and coins ($200), securities, deeds, letters of

TABLE 4-1
Policy Choices for Property Insurance

You	Personal Property	Dwelling
As a renter	Homeowner #4 Form *1 Personal Articles Floater *2 (high-value items) Personal Property Floater *2 (high-value items)	N/A
As a homeowner	Homeowners #3 Form *1 Homeowners #5 Form *2 Package Policies *2 Personal Articles Floater *2 Personal Property Floater *2	Homeowners #3 Form *2 Homeowners #5 Form *2 Package Policies
As a condominium owner	Homeowners #6 Form *1	N/A
As a renter	N/A	Dwelling Building(s) Special Form *2

*1 Key to perils
1. Fire and lightning
2. Damage to property removed from house (for a period of time not to exceed five days) if endangered by fire
3. Damage from water and chemicals used to extinguish fire
4. Windstorm and hail
5. Explosion
6. Riots and civil commotion
7. Damage by aircraft
8. Damage by vehicles other than those owned and operated by people covered in policy
9. Damage by smoke
10. Vandalism and malicious mischief
11. Theft
12. Damage from falling objects
13. Weight of snow, ice, sleet
14. Collapse of part or all of building
15. Damage from steam heating system or appliance for heating water
16. Water or steam leakage or overflow
17. Freezing of plumbing, heating, air conditioning
18. Short circuit injury to appliances and such
    *2 All risk

credit, passports, tickets, stamps, watches, gems, jewelry, furs, and watercraft including trailers ($1,000), guns ($2,000), and silverware ($2,500).

There are two types of deductible clauses in homeowners policies. The simpler option is to choose an amount between $100 and $500 that is applied to all perils.

The alternative is called *declining deductible*. This provides a $100 deductible for damages by windstorm or hail. If the loss is between $100 and $500, the company will pay 125 percent of that loss in excess of $100. If the damage exceeds $500, there is no deductible; the company pays everything. As you can see, the amount you must pay decreases as the loss increases. With this choice you agree to handle a large part of small losses, but protect yourself from any out-of-pocket expenses if you suffer a large loss.

To see how the math works in a declining deductible case, assume that a windstorm causes $300 damage to your home. First deduct $100. Then multiply the $200 balance by 125 percent to get $250. Your insurance company would pay $250 of the $300 loss.

You may want to consider adding a theft coverage extension endorsement to the basic coverage. This endorsement provides coverage for personal property that is stolen from your car even if there are no signs of forced entry. Without signs of forced entry, that property would not be covered in the basic policy.

Six Types of Homeowners Policies

Homeowners insurance policies differ in the range and nature of perils covered, the maximum benefits allowed, and minimum coverages (forms HO-1, HO-2, HO-3, and HO-6 limit minimum coverage to $8,000, HO-5 to $15,000, and HO-4 to $5,000). Below we have listed the primary features of each type of homeowners policy.

Homeowners basic form (HO-1) is quite limited. For example, fire coverage excludes loss of electrical appliances, fixtures, and wiring if the damage is caused by anything but lightning. Coverage for any smoke damage specifically excludes smoke from a fireplace. The policy does not cover damage resulting from water pipe breakage. Broken glass is covered only up to $50, and even that is void if the residence is vacant for more than 30 days. Other exclusions include accidental collapse of your building and damage from sonic booms. The list goes on, so be sure to look carefully if this is your choice.

Homeowners broad form (HO-2) covers all kinds of fire, smoke, and explosion damage. There is no limit on coverage for broken glass. Theft coverage is broader than under HO-1. HO-2 also covers damage done by vehicles to fences, walks, and driveways so long as the driver of the vehicle is not you or an occupant of your home. HO-1 excludes damage done by any vehicle.

Homeowners special form H0-3 combines broad-form peril coverage with all-risk coverage for your dwelling and detached structures. Damage to personal property covers falling objects from any source. Coverage for damage from vehicles is broadened to cover even you if you drive a vehicle into your house accidentally. Other things covered that are specifically excluded in HO-2 are loss or damage to television antennas, awnings, and outdoor equipment. HO-3 is the most popular of these packages. It affords the broadest coverage for the price.

Homeowners contents broad form (HO-4) is for renters. It covers unscheduled personal property and provides for additional living expenses due to loss. The only difference between the homeowners contents broad form (HO-4) and the homeowners broad form (HO-2) is that HO-4 covers everything under the category of vandalism and malicious mischief, even if the place is unattended for 30 days or longer. Any additions or alterations to your home can be covered up to 10 percent of the policy's face amount.

Homeowners comprehensive form (HO-5) offers the broadest coverage available among all these alternatives for your home and unscheduled personal property. HO-5 extends all-risk coverage to your personal property as well as your home and detached structures. For example, your personal property is covered against earthquake damage. Glass breakage coverage is expanded to include mirrors. Of course, there is a tradeoff for this more comprehensive coverage. The premiums are as much as twice those of other policies.

Condominium-unit owners coverage (HO-6) is similar to HO-4 (the renters policy) in that it covers unscheduled personal property, additions and alterations made by the unit owner, and living expenses. This policy goes a step further by covering your unscheduled personal property if you rent the condo. Through additional endorsements, you can get coverage for any loss assessment that you as a condo owner may be liable for.

Package Policies

Increasingly in recent years, the trend has been toward package policies which offer broad coverages at lower prices. These policies offer one liability limit (usually $1,000,000) covering all liability situations regardless of where they occur. Such a policy would probably cover gaps in coverage if you had separate homeowners and auto policies.

Also, these policies offer higher limits on scheduled (specifically identified) high-value property. They offer limits of $500 to $15,000 for each category of high-value property such as antiques, jewelry, furs, books, guns, and so on. All-risk coverage is extended from the dwelling to all unscheduled personal property. And the actual replacement cost of your house is guaranteed no matter what the face amount of the policy.

Package policies represent the wave of the future as insurance companies seek to cover families against risk rather than cover separate items of property.

Floaters

Floaters are basically personal property policies. There are two types: *personal articles* and *personal property*. Both protect against all perils except war, radioactive contamination, insects or vermin, and normal wear.

The personal articles floater (see Table 4-2) provides all-risk protection. It is also called a *schedule floater* because everything must be listed by class or article on the face of the policy along with the insuring conditions. For example, say you want to cover your golf clubs or scuba gear when they are in your car. In order to keep your premiums low, you might agree to policy stipulations that the items are covered only if your car or trunk were locked and there is clear evidence of forced entry. The more articles you want covered, the higher the premiums. With the many conditions, it is possible to custom-design a policy and premium.

The personal property floater offers protection on all articles of whatever value, scheduled or not, on a worldwide basis. There are three types of these policies. All of them are expensive.

Type 1 limits coverage on jewelry, watches and furs ($250 per occurrence); money ($100 per occurrence); and securities ($500 per occurrence).

Type 2 allows jewelry, watches, furs and other high-value property to be scheduled on the face of the policy and insured separately and arbitrarily for whatever amount you want.

Type 3 is similar to Type 1, except that furs may be insured against the dangers of fire and lightning for a larger amount.

Flood and Earthquake Insurance

Flood insurance is available through the National Flood Insurance program administered by the Federal Emergency Management Agency (FEMA) only to those homeowners who live in communities designated by the federal government. To find out if your community qualifies, ask your insurance agent.

Under this program, you can insure your home up to $185,000 for structural damage and up to $60,000 for contents damage and losses. Premiums vary according to FEMA's assessment of the risk of flooding for a particular area. More risk-prone areas obviously pay higher premiums. In 1988 the national average premium was approximately $240 per year for $65,000 in coverage.

In communities that have been designated as flood-prone, residents who fail to participate in the flood program are ineligible for the federal disaster relief

TABLE 4-2 Personal Articles Floater

Article or Class of Articles	Deductible or Special Conditions	Exclusions	Cost
Personal effects	$25 deductible (sometimes)	Money, passports, auto licenses, tickets, securities, baggage	$15 plus 1% of total insured value
Bicycle	$5 deductible	Damage from rust or mechanical breakdown	$10 per $100 of coverage
Camera			$1.65 per $100 of coverage
Fine arts		Damage from restoration or breakage of fragile objects	18¢ per $100 of coverage 15¢ per $100 if breakage coverage applies
Furs		Damage caused by moths or vermin	50¢ per $100 of coverage
Jewelry			$1.92 to $3.24 per $100 depending on the city and state
Musical instruments			Nonprofessional: 65¢ per $100 of coverage Professional: $3.50 per $100 of coverage
Silverware		Pencils, pens, articles of personal adornment, smoking implements	50¢ per $100 of coverage
Sports equipment		Loss due to failure of people to return equipment you loaned to them	$1.40 per $100 of coverage
Stamp and coin collections	$250 limit on any one stamp or coin		Stamps: 60¢ per $100 of coverage Coins: $1.75 per $100 of coverage
Wedding presents	Covered before wedding and 90 days afterward	Damage from breakage of fragile objects	13¢ per $100 of coverage 25¢ per $100 if breakage coverage applies
Food freezer	Food in family freezer covered if power goes off		$1 per $100 of food

Source: Insurance Services Office for California.

sometimes authorized after a severe flood. If you live in an area where flooding occurs, it is important to check this out.

When buying or building a home, you should be aware that homes built over water or below the high tide line are ineligible for flood insurance. So are unanchored mobile homes in some areas.

Earthquake insurance is written as an addition to a fire or homeowners policy. In some states, minimum premiums on earthquake policies are as low as 30 cents per $1,000; in other states, they are about $1.50 per $1,000. The standard deductible is 5 percent of the replacement cost of the home.

In California, insurance companies which offer homeowners policies are required to offer earthquake coverage. Californians buy about two-thirds of all earthquake policies.

Understanding the Fine Print

There are primarily three different clauses that may be attached to some policies:

1. The *other insurance clause* protects insurance companies from having to pay more than the damaged property is worth. For example, if you bought three policies on your home, thinking you would triple the payoff if something happened, this clause provides that no matter how many policies you hold the insurance company will pay only its share of the damage. If you have two policies with equal coverage limits on your home, each company would only pay one half of any damage that occurs. Insurance is designed to provide protection not a profit opportunity for policyholders.

2. The *mortgage clause* protects the bank or person who holds the mortgage on your property by promising to pay the full amount of the mortgage in the event of loss of the property. Primary promoters of this kind of insurance are the banks and savings and loans that make mortgages. Once the mortgage is paid off, this clause is no longer applicable.

3. The *leasehold clause* covers renters for damages to any physical improvements they make on the property while leasing it. For example, say you repainted the kitchen or built bookshelves for the living room at your own expense. If a fire or other covered hazard destroys your house or apartment, you can be reimbursed for damage done to those improvements.

Making a Claim

The first thing you should do after damage has been done to your property is to *call your insurance company*. Your agent can tell you what you are and are not covered for. The agent will advise you how to proceed with your claim.

Of course, you need to make a reasonable effort to minimize any loss. For example, if a lock has been broken you should get it fixed. If a window has been shattered, board it up until it can be replaced. Be sure to keep receipts for any expenses incurred in taking these preventive measures.

Once you have done what you can to prevent any further damage, it is a good idea to take pictures of the damage. Sit down and write your insurance company a letter detailing the damages and losses. Timing and facts in writing are very important factors in making a claim.

In the case of a burglary, call the police as soon as possible. They will probably send an officer to your home to make a report even though they may not be able to do anything about it.

In making your claim you will be able to refer to your detailed room-by-room inventory (won't you?!). After a burglary it is not unusual to find something gone that you had not noticed initially. To help your claim, check your records for purchase receipts for damaged or stolen articles.

You and your insurance company may not always agree on the settlement of a claim. In this case, either you or the company may demand that the issue be settled by an *arbitrator*. An arbitrator is an impartial third party who will listen to both sides and then render a decision.

If your claim is sizable and/or the difference with your insurance company is large, you may want an attorney to represent you. Your attorney will present your case to the arbitrator. Your insurance company will be represented by either a claims adjuster or an attorney depending on the issues involved. It is all carried on with an eye to a just settlement, though it can feel very much like a trial. After all, it does engender anxiety and major expense (attorney fees are typically one third of the total settlement). However, if the stakes are high enough, it may be worth the effort, both monetarily and in personal satisfaction.

Money-Saving Tips

We suggest that you talk with your agent about your present policy and if necessary change it. Even then, don't be overly complacent. It pays to keep alert to changes in your circumstances. You should keep in touch with your insurance agent regularly. In today's competitive insurance world, there are always many changes occurring in the types and prices of coverages offered.

You can save money by having a policy with higher deductibles. Be sure, though, you can afford the cash outlay if you need it. Set aside a reserve amount if you have any doubts.

You may save even more on your premium if you have smoke detectors, a sprinkler system, deadbolts on your doors, and safety locks on your windows. Some companies offer discounts for installing a burglar alarm system or buying a fire extinguisher. And saving premium dollars is not the only benefit. You may also gain a greater peace of mind.

And remember, just as with auto insurance, rates for the same coverage vary widely from company to company. Shop around. Be sure to ask your agent if there have been any changes in coverage or premium policies. Sometimes parent companies may lower a rate, but your agent may automatically renew you at the old rate if you don't check with him or her.

You may be able to get a price break if you buy all your insurance from the same company. An agent who knows you well should be able to more closely tailor your insurance coverages to your particular circumstances and eliminate duplication of coverage.

WRAPPING UP

In this chapter you have learned what property you can insure. Of course, it may be prohibitively expensive to insure everything you can insure, so you must make a decision on what you want to insure. Your personal property inventory will help you narrow that down as well as provide invaluable help in case of a loss.

You have learned that the difference between market value and replacement cost can be significant. For most people and situations, replacement cost coverage is the preferred option, even though it may cost 10 percent to 15 percent more.

You have learned the importance of keeping your house fully insured, so that you are not penalized by a loss which is only part of your house. And finally, you have seen that while there are a confusing number of policy options, only a few policies really are suitable for most people.

You know that advance preparation is your best protection from adverse developments. Dealing with an insurance agent does not have to be an unpleasant and frustrating exercise. In fact, once you understand the elements of property insurance, your visit with your agent will pay you dividends in terms of lower anxiety and peace of mind, no matter what the future holds.

CHAPTER 5

HEALTH INSURANCE

Even though inflation turned sharply lower in the 1980s, medical costs continued to skyrocket. A single day in the hospital in 1988 cost an average of $640, excluding doctors' bills! The charges for surgical procedures are staggering. A coronary bypass operation costs upwards of $25,000. A kidney transplant runs over $75,000. The average bill for inpatient, drug- or alcohol-abuse treatment runs over $12,000.

With figures like these it is easy to understand why we say that the most important checkup you can do is on your health insurance coverage. You know the old saying, "If you have your health, you have everything." If you can afford only one insurance, that insurance should be for your health. An extended illness means not only huge medical bills, but also the loss of your earning power. Just paying off these bills can put you in debt for years to come.

As we told you in previous chapters, the key to disaster management is preparation. If you become ill or disabled *before* buying health or disability insurance, you would probably be ineligible for it. That is why it is critical to make plans now for dealing with future contingencies.

On the other hand, don't let the fear of rising medical costs rush you into buying the first plan offered to you. Medical insurance coverage varies widely in costs, coverage, and usefulness. In this chapter you will learn how to tell whether you have adequate medical expense coverage. You will see the importance of protecting your income stream in case you become disabled. Selecting the right coverage can mean a big difference in today's dollars (premiums) as well as potential future dollars (benefits) if you do need to make a claim.

DETERMINING YOUR MEDICAL INSURANCE NEEDS

Despite efforts to control costs by both government and private insurers, the price of medical care continues to outstrip the inflation rate. Such rapid increases make it difficult to determine a maximum value on the medical costs you could face. It is nearly impossible to put a figure on the economic value of your family's health or the potential costs of both medical care and disability if a family member's health became impaired. With property insurance, calculating the coverage you need is a fairly straightforward process. Even with liability insurance, you know that if you insure for your current net worth plus future anticipated earnings you can be protected.

When dealing with medical costs you can make an educated guess as to how much you could reasonably afford to spend on medical expenses before incurring financial hardship. Just take a look at your personal balance sheet (a listing of your assets—such as savings, investments, and possessions; and your liabilities—such as debts, including mortgage). Remember, you can use your cash reserves to pay for small medical bills and save on premium dollars.

For example, identify the types of medical expenses that will occur regularly, such as physicals. Since you know both the frequency and cost of these expenses, you can plan to set aside money to fund them. In many cases this makes better sense financially than spending money on medical insurance that provides first dollar coverage.

The high cost of medical insurance premiums can be reduced if you take a higher deductible. Just as with your collision coverage, look at this as self-insuring for those amounts you can afford. The money you save by selecting a higher premium can be used to buy higher maximum coverage to protect you from a real catastrophe.

Prepayment and Indemnity Plans

Once you have identified those regularly occurring expenses, you need to confront the fact that there are many types of medical expenses that are impossible to predict. No one knows when he or she will be involved in an accident (isn't that why it's called an "accident"?). When you survey the various policies available to you, think in terms of catastrophe and possible bankruptcy from major health problems.

Distinguish between true health insurance plans and those that are merely prepayment plans. Prepayment plans are really just a type of savings plan to cover expenses that are almost certain, such as vaccinations or annual physicals. With these programs, you wind up paying not only the cost of the medical service but also the company's costs including the agent's commissions and expenses in servicing the claim. You could put that extra money to work for you buying true insurance coverage.

Another pseudo-insurance program that is widely advertised and heavily sold is an indemnity plan. The most common are hospital indemnity plans. You have probably seen the ads promising something like: "$100 a day for every day you're hospitalized, regardless of any other health coverage you have in force." The problem with these plans is that they don't pay anything when you incur large nonhospital medical expenses. They also have nothing to do with the actual cost of hospitalization.

Typically, indemnity plans are laced with restrictions that are not so boldly trumpeted. They generally pay out a smaller portion of their premium dollars in benefits than do broader coverage policies. Often they only cover one type of problem like cancer. Our advice is to forget them. There are far better uses for your insurance dollars.

Types of Medical Plans

There are two major types of medical insurance plans: *fee-for-service* and *prepaid care.* Fee-for-service coverage plans reimburse you for medical expenses incurred. In reality, what usually happens is that you assign payment direct from the company to the provider of your medical care. With fee-for-service you basically trade the chore of dealing with insurance forms for the freedom to select your own physicians.

Prepaid care plans have gained in popularity in recent years as a result of skyrocketing medical costs and legislative initiatives. Most commonly known as HMOs (health maintenance organizations), they provide complete medical care for a set annual or monthly premium. Care is generally rendered in a clinic-like setting rather than in an office. The main objection to HMOs is that you often are not able to see the same doctor each time you require care. We discuss HMOs and various permutations of the concept in more detail later.

Fee-for-Service Plans

Table 5-1 outlines the major features of each of five types of *fee-for-service* medical coverage. However, for the most part, the specialized coverages—hospital expense, surgical expense, and general medical expense plans—have given way to the two dominant medical plans: *major medical* and *comprehensive medical.* We will concentrate on delineating the major features of these two plans. Most people (approximately two-thirds) are covered under group insurance plans offered by their employers. Group plans are usually for comprehensive medical expense coverage, though federal law now mandates that an employer of 25 or more workers who offers fee-for-service insurance must offer HMO coverage as an option if one is located nearby. The trend seems to be moving toward HMOs, though they have not provided the savings for employers that were initially expected.

Major medical insurance covers nearly all types of medical care and expenses including hospital room and board, treatment by physicians and surgeons, psychiatric care, anesthesia, radiology, physiotherapy, nursing care,

TABLE 5–1 Types of Medical Expense Coverage

Type of Coverage	Items Covered*	Items Not Covered*	Range of Benefits (per occurrence)			Remarks
			Time	Money	Deductible	
Hospital expense	1–10	23–29	30 days to 2 years	$10 and up per day room and board; $10,000 expenses	$25 to $1,000	Most popular plan
Surgical expense	11	Anything not stated on schedule of operations		$300 to unlimited per operation	At discretion of insured	Usually attached to hospital expense coverage as rider
General medical expense	12–14	23–24	50 to 100 days	$5 to unlimited per day; total limit $250 to $500	At discretion of insured	Little more than a prepayment plan
Major medical	1–22	23–33	1 to 3 years	$10,000 to unlimited	$100 to $1,000	10 to 25% of all expenses to be paid by the insured in addition to deductible of his or her choice
Comprehensive medical (group plan)	All expenses	23–28	1 to 3 years	$25,000 to unlimited	$100 to $500	10 to 20% of all expenses to be paid by the insured in addition to a deductible

*Key to expense coverage
1. Hospital room and board
2. X-rays
3. Drugs
4. Laboratory examinations
5. Dressings
6. Physiotherapy
7. Maternity (including complications)
8. Mental disorders
9. Nursing expenses, in hospital
10. Nursing expenses, outside hospital
11. Operations
12. Doctor's home visits
13. Doctor's office visits
14. Doctor's hospital visits
15. Crutches
16. Splints
17. Blood and blood plasma
18. Braces
19. Prosthetics
20. Oxygen
21. Radiology
22. Rental of oxygen equipment, wheel chairs, hospital beds, and iron lungs
23. Anything not recommended or approved by a legally qualified physician
24. Injury sustained before the initial date of policy
25. Injury or illness due to war, declared or undeclared
26. Injury sustained while on active duty
27. Self-inflicted injury
28. Dental work
29. Eye examinations
30. Cosmetic surgery
31. Illness due to narcotic addiction
32. Illness due to alcoholism
33. Health examinations
34. Travel expenses (not ambulance)

laboratory examinations, maternity expenses, drugs, medicines and blood plasma, casts, splints, braces, crutches, artificial limbs, rental of oxygen equipment, wheelchairs, and hospital beds. In recent years, coverage has been extended to family counselors, chiropractors, podiatrists, and social psychologists (if medically necessary).

Major medical typically covers a fixed percentage of all expenses. There are usually limits on charges for room and board, extended care, private nursing, and outpatient psychiatric treatment. Group policies normally have a single lifetime maximum covering all types of injuries. These limits range from $250,000 to unlimited. If your policy has an *automatic restoration clause* these limits restore themselves by $1,000 to $5,000 per year if no benefits are required during the year.

Another restriction of some policies is a time limit. This means that the insurance company will only cover medical expenses incurred within one to three years of the date of injury. For example, if you break an arm in an accident, the company will only pay for expenses accumulated in the following year (or whatever limit is specified in the policy) which are the result of that one accident.

Deductibles play an important role in the cost of major medical coverage. They can be as low as $100, though the most common are $500, $750, or $1,000. The higher the deductible, the lower the premiums, all other things being equal.

In addition to deductibles, most major medical policies also have a *coinsurance feature*. This simply means that the company requires the insured to pay from 10 to 25 percent of all the eligible expenses in excess of the deductible amount. For example, assume you have a policy with a $500 deductible and a 20 percent coinsurance charge. If you incur $1,500 for that broken arm, you would pay $700 of the total bill ($500 deductible plus $200; 20 percent × $1,000).

Most group major medical plans have a *stop-loss limit*. This means that the portion of medical bills you have to pay is limited to the first $2,500 to $10,000 of covered expenses. Above this specified level the plan pays 100 percent. For example, with the same policy above with a $2,500 stop limit, if you incurred medical bills of $12,500, your out-of-pocket would be limited to $2,500 and the company would pay all the rest.

Major medical is the most important coverage you can buy. It also is the most widely available coverage for individuals. If you are not covered by a group health plan, you should get major medical coverage on your own.

Some policies spell out maximum benefits for each illness. Be sure that is at least $100,000 per person per hospitalization period and $25,000 per year for other medical expenses. If there is a lifetime maximum, make it as high as you can afford ($500,000 or more). Remember, you can reduce premiums by raising your deductible. These figures may seem outrageous, but it will only take one hospital stay to convince you of their practicality!

Comprehensive medical expense coverage has two key components. *Basic coverage* typically pays hospital and doctor bills with either a set dollar or time (in the case of hospitalization) limit. The second component is *major medical coverage.* It picks up where basic coverage leaves off. Table 5-2 gives an example of comprehensive expense coverage as it relates to a sample major medical plan.

Typical policies provide coverage up to $250,000 or more (after the deductible, of course) and your portion of the bills as stated in the coinsurance clause. The major medical coverage portion of a comprehensive policy is very much like the separate major medical coverage we detailed above. The high expense of comprehensive policies for individuals, however, limits this coverage primarily to group policies.

Fee-for-Service Providers

Blue Cross (hospitalization) and *Blue Shield* (surgical and general medical) are the largest fee-for-service single health expense plan providers in the nation, selling almost half of all privately issued health insurance. If you are a member you may go to any doctor or hospital (except true HMOs) to receive treatment. You only need to show your membership card. Usually the medical facility bills the provider directly. In those cases where the service rendered to you is not covered or only partially covered by your plan, you will be required to pay for the services yourself.

In many states these nonprofit organizations operate independently, offering their specialized services. In other states they cooperate in issuing joint plans for comprehensive medical care.

The traditional insurance sold by fee-for-service providers pays for specified medical procedures. As we indicated above, expenses which meet the "usual, customary, and reasonable" test are reimbursed. This policy is based on fees charged in your area. If you are billed for fees higher than the provider pays, they are usually higher than fees generally charged for the same services in your area. You may want to talk to your doctor or ask the provider to intervene on your behalf.

Commercial insurers are private companies that sell medical insurance coverage but are not associated with Blue Cross or Blue Shield. They account for about 40 percent of the market. They are both mutual companies (owned by policyholders) and stock companies (owned by shareholders). These companies show a willingness to tailor their policies to meet the needs of individuals and groups.

TABLE 5–2
Comprehensive Medical Expense Coverage

Policy Benefits	Expenses	Base Insurance Pays
Base insurance		
Hospital benefits		
Room and board in semiprivate room for up to 365 days	$4,500 ($250/day × 18 days)	$4,500
X-rays, lab, medicines, and such, up to $500	$2,000	$ 500
Surgical expense (according to schedule, $2,500 maximum)	$3,500	$2,500
Physician's expense ($15/day for 50 weeks)	$2,000 ($40/visit × 50 visits)	$ 750
Total	$12,000	$8,250

		Major Medical Pays	You Pay
Major medical			
80% of first $10,000 of covered expenses	(same expenses as above)	$2,920 (80% × $3,650*)	$730 (20% × $3,650*)
100% of all expenses above $10,000			$100
$100/calendar year deductible			
Total	$12,000	$2,920	$830

*Expenses not covered by base insurance ($12,000 − $8,250 = $3,750) minus deductible ($100) equals amount covered by major medical ($3,650).

It is impossible to comment on the general quality and types of coverages offered by any provider because of the great diversity available. There are both very high quality companies offering needed policies and others that sell primarily narrowly defined or indemnity policies that do not provide a good return for your insurance dollars. However, it can be said that their premium prices are generally higher than similar coverage provided by group plans or HMOs in those dwindling cases where they still offer individual policies.

Health Maintenance Organizations

Health Maintenance Organizations (HMOs) provide complete medical treatment in return for monthly or annual premiums. This prepaid alternative to fee-for-service plans covers most doctor and hospital care without the bother of filling out insurance claim forms. Unlike fee-for-service plans, an HMO is both the insurer and the provider of services. The thrust of HMOs is to offer efficient and effective health care to people directly rather than reimbursing them for care after the fact.

The Health Maintenance Act of 1973 established strict requirements for federally qualified HMOs (a designation needed for many government programs). They must provide comprehensive benefits, guarantee open enrollment periods for specific times during the year, and buy insolvency insurance to protect policyholders in the case of bankruptcy. As we mentioned above, those HMOs which meet these requirements qualify as alternatives to fee-for-service plans offered by employers.

Membership has grown to over 31 million members nationally in over 275 HMOs. However, that is still only about 6 percent of workers having employer-sponsored health plans. Many experts believe that those numbers will increase handily in the coming years.

There are two types of HMOs: a group-staff approach and the individual practice arrangement (IPA). A group-staff HMO provides services at one or more locations with salaried physicians. Patients typically pay a small fee ($1 to $5) per visit and receive comprehensive care. The most frequent complaint about HMOs is the impersonal service atmosphere that this approach often creates. It is frequently difficult for you to see the same doctor regularly.

IPAs have developed as a direct response to this complaint. An IPA contracts with private physicians who maintain their own offices. The doctors are paid on a discounted fee-for-service basis. Members are able to choose from a variety of participating doctors who then become their family physicians.

Also called *hybrid* HMOs, by 1988 IPAs had become the fastest growing segment of the HMO industry. While members are encouraged to use doctors and hospitals in the network, (they then have to pay little or nothing for their medical care), they can seek medical care outside the network if they want. However, they then must pay a higher fee or deductible.

One distinct advantage of HMOs is that they usually have programs to encourage members to seek preventive treatment. Many HMOs conduct classes on stress management, weight reduction, family planning, child care, and other related areas of health maintenance.

There are other advantages with HMOs. Monthly dues are low, visits are normally unlimited, and charges are nominal for medicine and laboratory work. Test duplications are avoided, thereby keeping costs lower. Doctors are financially motivated to work efficiently. They have immediate access to a patient's overall health records.

HMOs are not without their critics though. Some suggest that since doctors know the amount they will receive from each patient by his or her annual fee, they will do only the minimum necessary to keep a patient enrolled in the program.

However, keep in mind that members ultimately control their HMOs. They determine the level of benefits and fees. They also hire the doctors. It is unlikely they would inflict inferior care on themselves intentionally.

Making the choice between a fee-for-service insurer or an HMO is a very personal decision. You should weigh the estimated savings on the cost of medical services you would have to pay with the fee-for-service program (deductibles plus 10 to 25 percent of the balance) versus the higher monthly premium that HMOs normally cost. HMOs may be a better choice for families with young children because their expenses with frequent visits to the doctor are likely to be higher with a fee-for-service insurer.

Preferred Provider Organizations

Preferred Provider Organizations (PPOs) are providers of medical services rather than insurers. They are organizations of doctors and hospitals that offer their services to employers, unions, or insurers at good discounts. An employee who chooses the PPO option offered by an employer will usually still be able to utilize non-PPO services at a higher price.

For example, if you choose the PPO option and use its services exclusively you will have only nominal expenses. If you elect to use a non-PPO doctor for some reason, you will have to pay anywhere from $150 to $300 of the initial charges and 20 percent (or some other percentage) of all other medical bills arising from treatment by the non-PPO doctor.

PPOs are the new kid on the block as far as medical care goes. It is impossible to make any broad assessment of the quality or character of the medical care. If you are considering a PPO, we recommend you talk with people who have used the service.

Medicare

Medicare is the Social Security program that provides for medical coverage for people 65 and over. Medicare is a hot political subject. Since the coverages and policies undergo virtually constant change, you should check with a Medicare official or your insurance agent to get the very latest details.

There are two parts to Medicare coverage. Part A is the hospital plan. It is paid for through the Social Security taxes you pay while working. It covers hospitalization for benefit periods of 90 days. During the first 60 days of each benefit period, Medicare pays for all but $520 of the total cost. For the next 30 days it pays all costs above $130 per day.

New benefit periods can begin after you have been out of the hospital for 60 days. Between benefit periods there is a lifetime reserve of 60 days. This reserve pays bills above $260 per day. All doctors' bills come under Medicare's Plan B coverage, whether or not they are incurred during hospitalization.

Medicare's Plan B is optional medical insurance. It is paid for in part by premiums from those who choose to participate. For those receiving Social Security checks, the premium can be deducted automatically. To select Plan B coverage you must apply within three months of your 65th birthday. Otherwise you can join only in the first three months of any calendar year thereafter.

For people over 65, this is probably the least expensive insurance available since the federal government matches your premium payments dollar for dollar. In Plan B you pay a deductible and 20 percent of the balance of the approved amount. Medicare dictates how much it will pay doctors for office visits, treatments, surgery, and all other procedures. If your doctor does not agree to accept this amount, you have to pay any overage.

There are numerous policies designed to fill the gap between Medicare benefits and total bills. Most group plans feature coverage that fits the bill. If your employer's group plan does not extend beyond your retirement, it is often possible to convert to an individual policy. When seeking insurance to cover the gap between what Medicare pays and what is charged, be sure to buy only policies that are specifically called *Medicare supplementary insurance*. This name can be used only for policies that meet or exceed federal minimum standards of coverage.

DISABILITY INCOME NEEDS

While most people are familiar with the concept and need for life insurance, few take the time to investigate coverage for disability. Yet the facts show that if you are under retirement age, disability for an extended period of time is far likelier than death. For example, at age 22 the odds are seven times greater that you will suffer a serious disability of three months or more than you are to die during the year. At age 30 the odds are 50 percent that you will be laid up for three months or more before age 65. At age 42, your chance of suffering a serious disability before reaching 65 is three times greater than that of dying.

Disability insurance provides income while you are out of work due to an injury or illness. As you would expect from the high odds mentioned above, disability insurance is not cheap. For a 30-year-old the rates run about $15 to $30 a year for every $100 of monthly coverage. For example, if you need $3,000 per month to meet your regular expenses, the annual premium would run from $450 to $900. Rates jump much higher as you grow older. The same coverage for a 40-year-old can run as much as $1,500 to $2,000.

While many employers offer some type of disability coverage with their group plans, these often fall far short of what you really need. Typically, they will pay no more than 60 percent of your salary.

Self-Insuring for Income Loss

Your first thought may well be that your employer's sick leave policy will cover all you really need. But remember the statistics we listed above: disability periods of three months and longer are very possible. Few companies provide full pay for extended leaves.

By now you are familiar with the concept of self-insurance. When it comes to disability you can self-insure by determining how long you could support yourself in your present financial condition. It is possible and profitable (lower premiums) to use a waiting period before the policy starts making payments to you. The longer the waiting period, the lower the premiums.

For example, if you need $2,000 a month after taxes to pay normal living expenses, and you have $4,000 saved in an emergency fund, you can support yourself for two months. If your employer's sick leave policy will pay for one month, you can stretch out the waiting period for three months. Figure 5-1 illustrates typical savings that can occur through lengthening the waiting period.

The industry norm is 90 days. As a rule of thumb, trimming your waiting period to 30 days from 90 will cost you about 20 percent more. Stretching out the waiting period to one year will cut your premiums about 20 percent.

Other Types of Income Loss Protection

There are two main definitions of disability you need to know. Under the broadest definition of disability, income loss coverage (or salary continuation insurance) makes payments to the policyholder as long as the person is unable to perform *any or all* of his or her occupation. Under a strict definition of disabil-

FIGURE 5–1
Premiums Related to Length of Waiting Period

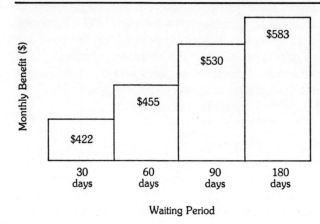

Amount of disability income that can be purchased for a $100 annual premium for a male, age 21.

ity, income loss coverage provides payments only if the insured can perform *no gainful* employment at all.

Traditionally, disability coverage insured the occupation rather than the disabled person's income stream. This new direction is aimed at motivating insureds to return to some type of employment without thereby sacrificing their entire insurance benefits. These *residual benefits* enable the insureds to receive partial payments if they return to work at a job that pays less than their previous salary.

Basic Contracts

A *basic contract* is the most popular form of disability income coverage. The policy may be written to cover total or partial disability due to accident or illness. These contracts vary widely from company to company because each adds or subtracts so many features to tailor it to the market it is trying to reach.

Basic contracts come in many varieties. There are three common clauses to understand before buying anything. *Presumptive disability clauses* specifically define the conditions under which the insured will be deemed disabled.

Double indemnity clauses guarantee that you will be paid twice as much if you have certain kinds of accidents that result in particular losses, for example, losing an arm in a particular type of accident. These are often couched in terms making them seem very lucrative, but who wants to make money losing parts of your body in specified ways? These are basically extra frills that really add no value. Never pay extra for this type of coverage. You are seeking income protection not another long-shot bet that you will insure yourself in the correct manner!

Prorating clauses enable the insurance company to raise the price of your insurance if your job changes or becomes more hazardous. The insurance company then has the right to increase its prices since its risk increases with the higher probability of you getting injured. Also this clause often limits payment to either your salary at the time of disability, or your average monthly salary over the few years prior to the disability, whichever is greater. It never allows for you to receive more than your salary at the time of disability.

Limited Contracts

Limited disability contracts impose restrictions beyond those of basic contracts. The most common type restricts coverage to a specific type of accident or disease. The most popular type of limited contract is the air-travel policy sold in many airports. Sold through coin-operated machines at airport terminals, coverage includes injuries sustained as a result of accidents while a passenger is on a scheduled U.S. airline or in transit to or from the airport via bus or limousine (but not taxi!).

There is a long list of payments for various bodily dismemberments that border on the ludicrous. Like rolling dice, if you hit certain combinations (such as an arm and a leg), you get double the amount of money. If you believe that your insurance needs should be approached with a Las Vegas gambler's attitude, then this is the right insurance for you. If on the other hand, you believe that your family needs to be protected for a certain amount to prevent financial hardship in case you are disabled, then there are far more intelligent ways to spend your insurance dollars.

Industrial Policies

Industrial policies provide coverage similar to basic contracts except in the amount and length of time the benefits are paid. These policies are sold individually. The amount of protection is usually considerably less than basic contract coverage. Premiums are typically paid weekly or monthly to an agent who comes to the insured's home.

A minimum waiting period of five weeks is usually imposed. The benefits are small. The major advantage of these policies is that it provides a means for people with low incomes and/or poor savings habits to obtain minimum short-term disability protection at a cost that is within their weekly budget.

The major disadvantage is that they are very expensive over the long term. The carrying, collection, and commission costs are so high that the benefits are smaller per premium dollar than for most other types of policies.

Determining Your Disability Needs

The thought of becoming disabled is less terrifying if you know that your financial future will not be disabled as well. While it is difficult to accurately estimate future medical expenses (you can never really know the full medical implications of an injury or illness), you can more accurately determine how much disability income you need. We have designed a worksheet, Action Paper No. 4, "Your Statement of Income Disability Needs," to help you make this calculation. In Figure 5-2 we've completed a sample Action Paper No. 4 to give you a better idea of how to complete the form yourself.

Use the blank Action Paper No. 4 from the Appendix at the back of the book. If you have completed a personal income statement such as those in other books in this series, use those figures to calculate your current annual living expenses. If you have not completed a personal income statement, you should do so as soon as possible. In the interim, you should be able to estimate your current living expenses by reviewing your checkbook for the last few months. How much do you spend each month on necessities—food, housing (rent or mortgage), clothing, utilities, and transportation (car payments and operating costs)? Multiply that by 12 months to get item 1 on Action Paper No. 4.

You then need to calculate what financial changes your disability will mean. First adjust those living expenses which will drop as a result of your disability. For example, if you are disabled, many insurance policies have provisions to waive premium payments while keeping your coverage in force. Also your tax bill will be lower if you are not receiving your normal wages. Disability payments are usually tax-free. Other expenses such as transportation and entertainment may also be lower. Enter the sum of these adjustments in item 2.

You probably will have some types of income still coming in. If you are married, your spouse may still provide income. There may be income you can count on from your investment portfolio in the form of dividends or interest or income from real estate rentals. Make appropriate entries for items 3 and 4.

In some cases, you may be eligible for Social Security benefits. However, don't count on them unless you are sure. Some 70 percent of all claims are denied. To qualify for Social Security disability benefits, your mental or physical condition must be severe enough to prevent you from doing *any* substantial work. The impairment must be expected to last at least 12 months or to result in death. And even if you meet these requirements, payments will not begin for at least five months after applying.

The size of the Social Security benefit payments is a percentage of your earnings over a period of years. Benefits may be payable at any age after you have earned a set number of dollars over a given period of time. The numbers change and the calculations are fairly complicated. It is best to check with your local Social Security office for exact details.

FIGURE 5–2
Sample Action Paper No. 4,
Your Statement of Income Disability Needs

Action Paper No. 4

Statement of Income Disability Needs

Name _Sample_

Date _____

1. Annual living expenses $ _30,000_

2. Adjusted annual living expenses

   Tax savings $ _3,000_

   Insurance premiums waived   _1,000_

   Other _____   _____

3. Spouse's income   _8,000_

4. Investment income   _1,000_

5. Social Security benefits   _4,400_

6. Total Adjustments (2 + 3 + 4 + 5) $ _17,400_

7. Net annual disability income needs (1 – 6) $ _12,600_

A number of states now have *temporary disability insurance* (TDI) programs. If you are eligible for state disability payments, include them in item 5. Then add items 2, 3, 4, and 5 to find out how much your living expenses will be reduced if you become disabled.

Then subtract item 6 from item 1 to determine your net annual disability needs. Unfortunately, once you have this figure there is still the problem that your needs may rise either due to changes in your family, such as another child, or inflation. Your disability insurance benefits will probably stay the same. That is the single greatest problem with obtaining enough disability coverage.

There are a number of things you could do if you anticipate increased living expenses. These include *reducing your financial obligations, buying a policy rider that affords automatic benefit increases each year, or buying a policy with sufficient limits to protect you from anticipated inflation.* The latter alternative, though, sounds simpler than it is. Most policies have restrictions that limit the maximum benefit payable to two thirds of your current monthly income.

Until you are able to build up your investable assets to give you sufficient cushion for periods of disability, it is probably best to buy the maximum coverage you are eligible for and can afford.

What to Look for When Buying Disability Coverage

Five companies—Paul Revere, Provident Life & Accident, Northwestern Mutual, Unum, and Monarch—sell about 50 percent of the high-limit disability insurance. Each insurance company tries to create its own special niche with special benefits written into their policies. As a result, you cannot just get directly comparable quotes from one company and then call the others to see what exactly comparable coverage will cost.

More than any other type of insurance, it is critical for you to *read the fine print* in your disability policy. Many disability income contracts include participation limits stating that no matter how many policies you own individually or under company plans, including Social Security or workers compensation, you can only be paid a percentage (often 80 percent) of your total compensation for all sources at the time of your disability.

With most long-term policies you are covered for life if your disability is a direct result of an accident. However, if you contract a debilitating illness like rheumatoid arthritis, coverage usually ends when you turn 65. In some cases it is possible to change that, but you will pay a higher fee.

Maximum benefits are usually two thirds of your salary or $6,000 per month, whichever is less. As mentioned above, waiting periods are usually 90 days but can be as much as one year.

Understanding the Clauses in Disability Insurance

When you go shopping for a disability policy, there are a number of important points you should clarify before making a final decision. While there is no reason to seek out the most expensive policy, there is certainly no guarantee that the least expensive will serve your needs beyond saving a few dollars today. Be sure to find out about each of the following elements:

1. *Waiting period.* This is the time period between the beginning of your disability and the start of benefit payments. This is the equivalent of a deductible for health or property insurance. Also called the *elimination* period in some policies, the important thing to remember is the longer the period, the lower the premium. However, your most important consideration is how long you can afford to be without the cash flow if you are disabled. The usual waiting period is 90 days but commonly is as short as 30 days or as long as one year.

2. *Benefit period.* This is the total time that benefits are paid once you begin to receive them. Benefit periods can be as short as one year and as long as your lifetime for disabilities caused by accidents. The longest benefit period for disability through illness is to age 65 for most policies. Obviously the longer the benefit period, the higher the premium. If you can strike a happy medium between lengthening your waiting period *and* your benefit period and still afford the premium, so much the better.

Your greatest financial risk is a lifetime disability, so that should be your goal with disability insurance. A one- or- two-year period may look attractive when you are in the peak of health, but remember, the whole idea here is to plan for the worst in exchange for the peace of mind it will bring you and your family.

3. *Premium and renewal guarantees.* The best situation here would be to get a *noncancellable, guaranteed renewable* policy. This means that you are assured of paying the same premium and the company can't cancel your policy. However, nothing comes free in the insurance business. These types of guarantees cost more. The security they offer may be worth the cost though. Be sure to compare the difference in premiums before you decide.

Other less desirable types of policies include *optionally renewable,* which can be renewed only at the option of the company. If your health deteriorates you may find your policy cancelled just when you may really need it.

Guaranteed renewable policies have to be renewed by the company at expiration time if you so request. Premiums may be changed but only if they are changed for everyone in your classification group (e.g., everyone in a particular geographic area). These policies cost more than optional renewal but less than noncancellable, guaranteed renewable policies.

4. *Definition of disability.* It is important to know in advance just how disabled you must be to collect on your policy. Nothing is as disheartening as finding out that your idea of disabled does not meet your insurance company's requirements. The most liberal definition states that you are entitled to full benefits if you cannot perform the *main functions* of your regular occupation. More restrictive language considers you disabled only if you are unable to engage in any occupation for which you are reasonably suited by education and experience.

For example, a trial lawyer who could no longer speak above a whisper would qualify under the first definition even if he or she could still earn an income performing other paperwork-oriented duties.

The least acceptable definition is one that considers you disabled only when you cannot engage in any type of work. While most policies provide for some type of payment in case of partial disability, many require that you undergo a period of total disability before you are eligible to collect partial benefits.

The definitions of partial disability vary. Some are related to income loss. Others are defined in terms of the physical handicap. The level of partial benefits in cases tied to income loss are usually figured at a set percentage of total disability benefits. For example, if you earned $3,000 per month before disability and now are able to earn only $900, you have suffered a 70 percent loss of income. If the maximum payment under the policy is $2,000 per month, you will be entitled to $1,400 ($2,000 × 70 percent).

If you are a service professional, seek out a policy with the most liberal definition of disability that applies until you are age 65. In less specialized work the more restrictive definition might be acceptable if the policy provides replacement of partial losses of income.

5. *Residual benefits.* Residual benefits refer to payments of partial benefits. For example, if you are only able to earn 50 percent of your former income, a policy with residual benefits will pay you 50 percent of the maximum benefits. As your working time or income increases, your benefit declines. Residual benefits should be included in any policy you are seriously considering.

6. *Cost-of-living (inflation) adjustments.* Failure of your benefits to increase as your living expenses rise is a major problem with most disability policies. It is important to get a policy which features automatic increases by a set percentage or that is tied to the rate of inflation (in other words, a *cost-of-living rider.*) Be aware that policies covering a set percentage of your salary essentially increase your benefits while you are well. Others adjust only while you are disabled. Be prepared to pay as much as 20 percent to 25 percent more for a cost-of-living rider.

An *option to purchase rider* permits you to buy additional coverage in the future without having to provide proof of insurability. With this guarantee you can ensure that your policy keeps up with your cost-of-living increases without having to rely on the insurance company to make the proper adjustments.

7. *Social Security supplement.* This extra provision in the form of a rider added to your policy provides for a payment either of a set amount—for example, $500—or an amount equal to what you would receive in Social Security benefits if you qualified. Once you actually do (if you do) begin to receive Social Security payments, this amount would be adjusted downward or eliminated. Typically, this will only kick in after you have been disabled for six months or longer.

8. *Coordination of benefits clause.* In order to prevent someone from making it profitable to become disabled by arranging to make more money not working than working, the coordination of benefits clause states the maximum disability income you may receive *from all insurance sources* (both government and private). The maximum is usually stated as a percentage of your current income such as 66 percent.

9. *Rehabilitation provisions.* As the insurance industry has focused more on rehabilitation, a number of policies provide for continuation of benefits while you are in a rehabilitation program. This provision thus ensures that you will not lose your benefits if you enter a work-related rehab program. Some policies even pay for tuition and equipment expenses for such programs.

GROUP HEALTH INSURANCE

Some two-thirds of Americans have group health insurance coverage through their place of employment. Their employers typically pay part or all of the cost. When you leave a job, you normally have a 30-day grace period to convert from the group policy to an individual policy with the same insurance company without having to pass a physical examination. Whenever you have an opportunity to buy group coverage, do it!

There are five types of group insurance:

1. *Group health expense coverage* is regularly available equally to all members of a general class of employees. There may be a waiting period at the beginning of employment. While policies differ, they generally are either major medical or, more commonly, comprehensive medical expense insurance. Most employers who offer fee-for-service plans now also offer HMOs as an alternative.

Be sure to ask about your major medical maximum coverage. Deductibles also vary widely, so you should clarify what your plan requires. If the maximum coverage or deductibles do not meet your expectations, consider supplementing the coverage. You will find that individual plans designed to supplement group coverage will be much less expensive than straight individual insurance.

2. *Short-term disability benefits* provide an employee with normal salary during sick leave (time taken off from work for legitimate illness). The longer you have worked for a company, the more sick days you usually accumulate.

3. *Long-term disability plans* are coordinated with Social Security and workers compensation. They generally pay benefits of about two-thirds the employee's salary. They usually begin from one month to two years after application. They typically continue in force to age 65. Each plan has maximum benefits. Many of them stop payments after two years if the beneficiary is able to work at *any* kind of job.

4. *Accidental death and dismemberment coverage* is voluntary for employees. It is paid in a lump sum if an employee loses a body appendage or is killed in an accident on or off the job. It is a form of double indemnity. We do not recommend that you buy it. There are far more practical uses for your insurance dollars.

5. *Dental insurance* is now quite common under group plans. In many respects it is similar to other kinds of health insurance; there are deductibles, maximum benefit limits, and copayment provisions. The major difference with dental plans is that they cover the cost of preventive care, like regular checkups and cleanings.

Preventive care is encouraged by most dental plans by offering 100 percent coverage for routine examinations and cleaning. Restorative treatments such as fillings, crowns, oral surgery and the like usually carry 50 to 80 percent coverage, depending on the specific treatment involved. Orthodontics is seldom covered by basic dental plans.

Duplication of Coverage

If you and your spouse work for different companies that both offer group medical and/or dental insurance, it pays to look over the coverage of both plans carefully. If you do not have children, and both plans are roughly equal, you can often save money by keeping separate plans. However, be sure to check the respective deductibles and copayment provisions before making your decision.

Most premiums are structured so that the lowest premium coverage is for only one person. But when you expand that to cover more than one, even if only your spouse, the premium usually goes up more than double the original level. That is because the *family* plan is designed to cover entire families. And you know that the average family has 2.5 children plus the parents!

It used to be that it was a good idea to keep double coverage with plans from both employers of a working couple. The idea was that one plan would pay 80 percent of the bills and the other could be used to fill the gap. However, most policies are now written to specifically prevent that approach. Now policyholders can be reimbursed only under one plan. That means your overall coverage is only as good as the best plan.

Shopping for the Best Values

No matter what coverage, you never want to spend more than necessary. However, as we have pointed out, don't base your decision solely on low prices. Health insurance comes in so many varieties with so many clauses and riders that can be added or subtracted that it is important for you to first get the coverage you need. Then comparison shop, but don't be deluded into thinking that all other things are equal. Be sure to ask specific questions about *policy*.

We have included Action Paper No. 5, "Shopping for Health Insurance" to help you do your shopping. Most policies now set a combined hospital and surgical limit. You should have a minimum of $500,000, and $1,000,000 is preferred. Group plans should cover 80 percent of home health care that is supervised by a doctor. Psychiatric care is looming as a more important element of coverage. Leading group plans provide for 100 percent coverage for up to 30 days of inpatient nursing and hospital services, 50 percent for outpatient therapy.

Medical Coverage

Other than age and health, the four major determinants of health insurance costs are the type and amount of coverage, length and term of policy, size of deductible, and provisions regarding renewal of the policy. In general, it is quite simple: the greater the deductibles and shorter the term, the smaller the premium. Lower the insurer's risk, and you lower your cost.

With medical expense coverage and hospital and surgical coverage, as with most things in life, you get what you pay for. The more comprehensive your protection, the costlier it will be when the bill arrives. If you have a large family or are accident-prone, HMOs offer the most for the money. Otherwise, major medical coverage will probably give you the greatest value.

In general, group policies offer the best coverage because of minimized operating costs. They are especially beneficial when the employer pays all or part of the premiums. An individual cannot duplicate this coverage for the same cost.

Disability Coverage

Since disability coverage is relatively expensive, it makes sense to carefully study ways you can save premium dollars. The most obvious way is to extend the waiting period as long as possible. However, don't extend it beyond what you can realistically afford just to save a few premium dollars today. If you are disabled, you will regret your past penurious ways. And not only that, if your disability is prolonged, your shortsightedness will probably cost you money. It hardly makes sense to save money so you lose money, does it?

If you either have or can reasonably expect to set aside a liquid emergency fund that also earns interest or dividends, this is the single best way to afford a longer waiting period. Statistics vary, but take our word for it, by careful planning you can save substantial amounts in premium dollars without risking the very thing for which you buy disability coverage.

If you have a large IRA account, keep in mind that federal law allows you to withdraw money without the 10 percent tax penalty if you are legitimately disabled. Count your IRA as part of your cash emergency fund in calculating how long you can wait before getting benefits.

Most companies allow you to add a *social security rider* to your policy. This effectively lowers the company's risk by allowing it to pay you less if you qualify and receive money from Social Security benefits. Normally, the rider is written so that the company can reduce its payments by whatever amount you receive from Social Security to a preset maximum. The company will guarantee a base amount of payment though, even if the combined benefits from both the plan and Social Security exceed the promised benefit.

WORKERS COMPENSATION

If you have an accident, are hurt, or become ill on the job, you will probably be eligible for coverage under state-mandated workers compensation insurance. Most states require that employers carry workers compensation insurance. However, not all workers are necessarily covered.

Workers compensation insurance is like no-fault insurance. Employers, through their workers compensation insurance carrier, assume responsibility for any illness or injury that is work related. The type and amount of benefits you are entitled to are set by state law. Normally, all your medical bills and a certain percentage of your wages up to a maximum amount are covered. The definition of what is and is not work related is steadily expanding to include such things as mental fatigue or other stress-related disabilities.

WRAPPING UP

If everything in life is a matter of priorities, then health should certainly be on your list of what's important to you and your family. Medical problems in this day and age of high medical costs will directly affect your financial well-being if you do not take steps to protect against unforeseen disasters. A prolonged illness may not only incur huge medical bills, but can tear down the financial security you work so hard to provide for your family.

Check Up on Yourself

☐ Identify routine medical expenses
☐ Estimate affordable deductible
☐ Accident proclivity is low/high
☐ Review living expenses
☐ Determine appropriate hospital insurance
☐ Verify yearly medical expenses

☐ Check emergency fund
☐ Want income loss coverage
☐ Consider residual policy
☐ Review disability contract
☐ Buy disability insurance
☐ Supplement group plan
☐ Know maximum lifetime coverage

Consider your needs scrupulously. Think in terms of the consequences of a major setback. If you can afford only one kind of health insurance it should probably be major medical coverage (or an HMO). It is vital that you understand exactly how you are protected and how you are not.

You can save money by avoiding needless duplication and using higher deductibles or waiting periods. Controlling cost both in terms of today's premium dollars and tomorrow's medical expenses is the main issue.

By this time you know more than you probably ever thought you wanted to know about health insurance! But hopefully you now understand the full implications of today's rising medical bills. Arranging appropriate coverage is not something that can be put off until tomorrow. Take our word for it, you need it now! Good health insurance is part and parcel of good financial planning.

CHAPTER 6

LIFE INSURANCE

When you think about it, "life" insurance is really a misnomer. What you buy or *should* buy is protection for your loved ones in the event of your death. In other words, you are buying "death insurance." While it may seem overly maudlin, the point does serve to emphasize the real issue that should concern you: whether and how much you need to provide for your dependents.

Unfortunately, this simple point is all too often lost in the advertising hyperbole that characterizes life insurance sales. There are over 600,000 salespeople who want to sell you insurance. Some approach their job with diligence, patience, and integrity. They know and understand that they are best served by providing their clients with long-term, carefully planned service and advice. On the other hand, there are those who are more interested in their share of the sales commission than in what is best for you.

Few of us want to dwell on the unpleasant. There are few thoughts more unpleasant than those of our own death. When most people sit down (or more frequently are dragged to the table kicking and screaming) to discuss life insurance with their agent, they simply do not have the necessary information to make informed decisions. Usually they wind up deferring to their agent's expertise: "What do you think is appropriate?" Is it any wonder that most Americans are either underinsured or simply incorrectly insured?

We believe that when it comes to insurance it is important to confront your own mortality dispassionately. Remove yourself from the emotional picture. You won't be around to experience it anyway! There should not be any great dilemma about when to buy life insurance, how much to buy, or a point missed by many, even whether to buy. It is all a matter of dollars and sense.

Generally speaking, if the dependents you leave behind won't need the money to survive on their own (e.g., your children have reached adulthood), or if you have no dependents, you do not need life insurance. Don't confuse your insurance needs with your speculative desires. The proper place for speculation is with investments where there is a chance for gain. The proper role of life insurance is to protect your family in case of your premature death. You insure against risks for which there is no chance for gain. You take risks to speculate because there is a chance for gain.

Uncomplicated is our guiding word for this chapter. While you may be confused by the seemingly endless maze of life insurance types and varied sales pitches, what you need to know is really quite simple. The key, as with other types of insurance, is to identify your particular needs.

In this chapter we show you how to resolve any dilemmas or misunderstandings you may have about your life insurance needs. We do this through an efficient, straightforward, eight-step evaluation of those needs.

As with our other chapters, you will learn here about policy variables and the types of policies available. We detail those important and sometimes misunderstood clauses that make up the contracts. And finally, we show you how to shop for the plan that will meet your needs.

DETERMINING YOUR LIFE INSURANCE NEEDS

If all you ever heard or read about life insurance was the advertising, you would think everyone needed life insurance. Why, it provides a tax shelter, an investment return, a savings plan, and oh yes, even insurance if you pass away. But the fact is, there are many people who simply do not need life insurance.

Children, most retirees, single people without dependents, and anyone who has achieved the financial means for his or her dependents to continue a given standard of living should he or she pass away prematurely, should *not* carry life insurance.

One of the great fables of our time seems to be the notion that life insurance is a good way to invest money. In fact, life insurance serves no purpose other than to take care of dependents in the event of your death.

Some insurance companies claim to offer policies with savings factors that are competitive with other investments. We believe that insurance policies are for disaster protection. There are far better investment vehicles available at far lower costs that can be employed to build your own treasure chest.

According to the American Council Of Life Insurance in 1988, the average household that had life insurance carried coverage of $81,200. At first glance that may seem a large amount. However, if you were able to invest that at 8 percent, you would only earn $6,496 per year. You couldn't live very well on that! While it is easy to assume that you can cut back on your standard of living, it is much more difficult to do than to say.

Even a sum as large as $100,000 can dissipate quickly if you must live on it almost exclusively. For example, $100,000 invested at a 4 percent *real* (adjusted for inflation) return will last only slightly more than 4.5 years if you must withdraw $2,000 per month for living expenses.

An Eight-Step Approach

This procedure is designed to help you determine your family's financial needs after your death. Before you can make an intelligent decision, you must analyze the elements that go into determining how much your family will need. You then must factor in the various sources of income you will have. Your life insurance should generate sufficient income to fill the gap that occurs between your family's cash needs and their other income resources.

To help you complete the eight-step procedure for identifying your needs, we have completed a sample worksheet (see Figure 6-1) for a man 35 years old earning $40,000 a year. His wife, a homemaker, is also 35. They have two young children.

We have included a separate column headed by "Your Family" right next to our sample family's figures in Figure 6-1. If you pencil in rough estimates for your own circumstances as we go through the sample worksheet, you will be better prepared for completing your own Action Paper No. 6, "The Eight-Step Procedure." A blank Action Paper No. 6 is located at the end of this book, in the Appendix. The following step-by-step instructions will help you.

Item 1. If your total estate (net worth from your balance sheet plus anticipated proceeds from any life insurance coverage you may already have, for example a group policy through your job or other potential proceeds such as a settlement from a spouse's pension fund) is less than $20,000, use $2,200 here. Our sample couple's total estate is between $20,000, and $200,000 so we entered $5,000 here. If your total estate is greater than $200,000 enter $10,000 on this line. The more valuable your estate is, the higher your estate taxes, funeral, and administrative expenses will be.

Item 2. Your balance sheet will detail your debts (liabilities). Your insurance coverage should pay off all of these with the exception of your mortgage. Enter the total amount you owe on everything else (this includes car loans, credit cards, bank debt, and so on). Our sample couple would need $2,500 to pay off their nonmortgage debt.

Item 3. Your contingency or emergency fund should cover your dependents' living expenses that do not stop for your dependents when you die. Two-months' take-home pay, or even a little more, is a good rule of thumb. Of course, the exact figure depends on your judgment and what you can afford to put aside. Our sample wage earner's take-home pay is $2,500 per month. The couple has set aside an emergency fund of twice that, or $5,000.

Item 4. The cost of putting your children through college rises steadily. Effective in 1985, college students over 18 became ineligible for survivors' ben-

FIGURE 6–1
Sample Action Paper No. 6,
The Eight-Stop Procedure

Action Paper No. 6

The Eight-Step Procedure

Name(s) _____ *Sample* _____

Date _____

	Sample	Your family
1. Funeral, administrative, and estate tax expenses	$ 5,000	$ _____
2. Debt resolution (excluding home mortgage)	2,500	_____
3. Contingency fund (twice your monthly take-home pay)	5,000	_____
4. College fund	76,800	
5. Net Annual Living Expenses		
a. Average annual living expenses	29,000	_____
h. Spouse's average annual income	$ 22,500	$ _____
c. Average annual Social Security	5,000	_____
d. Net annual income needs (a - b - c)	1,500	_____
e. Years until spouse reaches age 90	55	_____
f. Average annual investment rate factor (Table 6-1)	22	_____
g. Total Net Income Needs (d × f)	$ 33,000	$ _____
6. Total Monetary Needs (1 + 2 + 3 + 4 + 5g)	$ 122,300	$ _____
7. Total Investment Assets	$ 10,000	$ _____
8. Your life insurance needs (6 - 7)	$ 112,300	$ _____

efits under Social Security. Current data suggests that if you plan to send your child to a private school, expect a minimum cost of $9,600 per year for tuition, room and board. If you plan to send your child to a public school, use a figure of $4,900 per year. Our couple plans to send both their children to private colleges. Using our formula they will need $76,800 ($9,600 × 2 children × 4 years).

Item 5a. Given your present living expenses (see Action Paper No. 4, line 1), you can estimate average annual expenses for your spouse. Don't forget added child care and expenses that are now entirely yours. Our sample couple spends most of their income on fixed expenses such as mortgage, food, and clothing. Our estimate allows for a slight decrease in living expenses with one adult gone, but anticipates additional child-care costs.

Item 5b. If your spouse would return to work in case of your death, estimate his or her average take-home annual earnings. This will necessarily be quite subjective. Be conservative. In our example, the wife estimates that she could resume a professional career. She figures her annual salary would be about $30,000. She estimates that would translate into $22,500 after taxes.

Item 5c. If you qualify for Social Security (it depends on how long you work and how much you make) and have no children, enter $3,000 as the benefit to your beneficiary. If you have one child use $4,000. If you have two or more minor children, use $5,000 as our sample couple has done. These are simply estimates of the average benefits that would be paid to eligible recipients. To find out more accurately what benefits you and your survivors are entitled to, you should complete Form SSA 7004, Request for Statement of Earnings from the Social Security Administration. In 1988 the maximum monthly Social Security payout to a surviving spouse was $838. For a family the maximum was $1,834.

Item 5d. Subtract the sum of 5b and 5c ($22,500 + $5,000 = $27,500) from 5a ($29,000). Enter the result ($29,000 − $27,500 = $1,500) on 5d.

Item 5e. Assume your beneficiary will live to age 90. Subtract his or her present age from 90. In our example, the number of years is 55.

Item 5f Table 6-1 lists investment rate factors. The first column indicates the number of years until your spouse reaches age 90 (55 years in this case). Choose the investment rate factor which best describes your own approach. The conservative path assumes 2 percent annual *real* growth, using bank accounts and bonds for your primary investment vehicles. The more aggressive investment factor implies a 4 percent real annual growth rate using stocks and real estate. *Real* growth means that the figures have been adjusted for inflation and taxes. Our sample couple selected "more aggressive." Reading across the line at age 55 to the appropriate column gives an investment rate factor of 22 for them.

TABLE 6–1
Investment Rate Factors

5e Number	Conservative	More Aggressive
25	20	16
30	22	17
35	25	19
40	27	20
45	30	21
50	31	21
55	33	22
60	35	23

Item 5g. Multiply your family's net annual living expenses (line 5d) by the investment rate factor on line 5f. This number estimates the total net income needs of your family if you died today. For our sample family, that number is $33,000 ($1,500 × 22).

Item 6. Add the numbers in items 1, 2, 3, 4, and 5g to find your total monetary needs (how much money is required to meet your needs). Our couple's total monetary needs are $122,300 ($5,000 + $2,500 + $5,000 + $76,800 + $33,000)

Item 7. Your balance sheet will give you the current figure for your family's investment assets (savings, stocks, bonds, mutual funds, real estate, etc.). Enter here the amount of your liquid assets (those that can be converted to cash relatively easily and quickly). Our couple has $10,000 invested in common stocks and mutual funds that could be cashed in an emergency.

Item 8. Subtract line 7 from line 6. The result will give you a good idea of how much insurance protection you should buy. For our couple that amount is $112,300 ($122,300 − $10,000).

Decreasing Needs and Increasing Assets

Our goal throughout this book is to reduce feelings of vagueness and helplessness you might have about your financial well-being. What you have now, plus your earning power will determine your financial future. Insurance is one way to minimize risks to that future.

But insurance can't alter the fact that everyone experiences changes. Some of those changes will be beneficial and therefore welcomed. Others will not be of your own choosing, but nonetheless important. In the financial sphere, most of us experience virtually constant change throughout our lifetime. When you evaluate your insurance needs, it is crucial to understand just how your needs change. With this knowledge you can make financially rewarding decisions. Too often people are sold insurance that is wrong for them either because it does not do what they want or because the coverage they receive could have been purchased less expensively.

If you marry and have a family, your insurance needs will increase as your family grows. As time passes though, your total life insurance needs decrease because your spouse has an increasingly shorter life expectancy. His or her greatest financial needs, secure financial resources to provide essential living expenses, decrease accordingly. Your other beneficiaries, such as minor children, will finish school, reach adulthood, and no longer be dependent.

However, life does not always progress in quite the straightline manner described above. For example, funeral and administrative expenses increase as your estate grows. Large liabilities, like your home mortgage, usually come in the middle of your life and then decrease with time. While your children are growing, a college education fund will be an important part of your planning. But once they finish their education, that need disappears.

A young married couple with small children has a greater need for life insurance, because they must protect dependents over longer periods of time, than they will ever have again. This assumes that as they grow older their assets will increase but their dependents will not. The only smart way to buy insurance is to consider what would be needed if you were to die *right now*, not in ten years. You do not know what your needs will be then. Your lifestyle may change dramatically. Your family may grow. You may hit the lucky state lottery ticket. *Life insurance is of major importance only when your needs exceed your assets.*

The insurance industry is undergoing a dizzying pace of change. You need to reassess your life insurance coverage every year. New products are constantly being introduced. Old products are being changed. Prices are in a constant state of flux. Depending on changes in your particular circumstances, your needs may best be served by an entirely different type of policy than the one you have. Also, if your assets are increasing while your needs are decreasing, you may want to reduce your coverage to save money in premiums (see Figure 6-2).

More than likely you will outlive your need for life insurance. Once you retire or become financially independent there is little reason to continue paying for coverage you no longer need. And even if you believe that you do need life insurance coverage, your needs are certainly going to be dramatically different when you are retired. It pays to not pay for the same old policy without first checking over the variables. *The length of time you need coverage is the key variable in your decision-making.*

FIGURE 6–2
Decreasing Needs/Increasing Assets

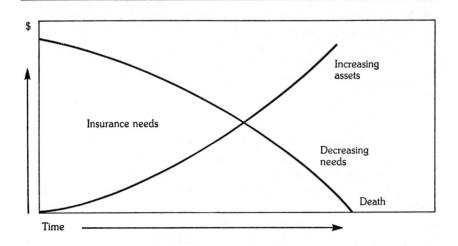

VARIABLES IN LIFE INSURANCE POLICIES

Comparing life insurance policies can be a frustrating, thankless job. The industry has not standardized policy provisions. The possible combinations seem infinite. Just narrowing the field so you can compare apples with apples is not as simple as you might expect. All this is certainly not aided by what some observers believe is an intentional attempt to confuse the matter so much that you must rely on the industry's salespeople!

However, even though there are more types of life insurance policies to choose from than most of us can or would care to count, and even though there is no such thing as a "standard policy," there are only five ways in which policies vary.

1. *Protection* for your dependents in case of your death. The amount of protection varies with the type of policy. This is the primary purpose of life insurance, though all too often this concept is lost in sales pitches about investment or tax shelter benefits.

2. *Savings*, which is the distinguishing feature of *cash value* insurance. In a cash value policy, part of your premium dollars go to pay for protection while the balance goes into a savings reserve (the cash value of the policy). At first, most of the premium pays for protection. Later, more of the premium goes to building up the cash reserve. We rarely, if ever, recommend this feature of life insurance.

3. The *face amount* of the policy, which is the amount payable at death. It may increase, decrease, or remain constant depending on the type of policy you select.

4. The *policy period*, which designates how long the policy will remain in effect. This can vary from a specific number of years to a lifetime. If it is for a specific term, there will be different types of renewability provisions that affect the premiums. For example, you want to be sure that you can renew the policy without need for a doctor's examination each time. We discuss renewability options in more detail later.

5. *Premiums*, which are what you pay for your policy. They may be paid for the entire term of the policy or may be paid for only part of the policy's life. There are many different payment plans. Your premiums may remain constant throughout or they may increase or decrease depending on the type of policy you have. They are based on the other four variables—protection, savings, face amount, and policy period—as well as your age and health.

Mortality tables play a major role in how insurance companies calculate premium charges. Mortality tables are simply statistics on how many people die at various ages. Even though people are living longer, companies are not required to point out that fact to long-term policyholders, even though new tables may result in lower rates.

Term Insurance: Pure Insurance

Despite the creation of many different types of life insurance policies, the primary division is still between *term* and *cash value* (also called permanent). All the varieties are really just different twists on these two concepts.

Term insurance is pure, unfettered financial protection for specific beneficiaries in the case of your death. Term insurance is issued for a set period of time. Term has no savings or cash value element. Compared to the many varieties of cash value insurance, term is straightforward and easy to understand. However, as you will see in the following discussion, there are still some differences, not the least of which is wide price disparity between issuers.

With term insurance, the insurance company will pay money only if you die. Like auto, property, or health insurance, it pays only if there is a loss. When companies issue term insurance they are betting on the odds. Since most people live beyond the period covered by their term insurance, nothing is paid on most policies. That is how the insurance companies make their money.

Term insurance provides the largest pure protection for the lowest premium. Historically, the main buyer of term insurance has been the father of a young family. Today, however, the buyer is equally likely to be a single mother or other single person who feels responsible for aging parents.

Rates for term insurance for people under 40 are dramatically cheaper than cash value. For example, in 1988 a healthy, nonsmoking 35-year-old could buy $1 million of term insurance for less than $1,000 per year. Rate breaks are generally available at $100,000, $500,000, and $1 million. Be careful about buying small amounts of term insurance. A $10,000 policy may appear cheap, "only a few cents per day," but if you compare the cost per $1,000 of coverage (the standard measuring stick for comparing term policies) the rate is exorbitant.

Renewable Term Insurance

Perhaps the most important feature of term insurance that you need to consider is the renewability conditions. It is easy enough to compare the rates of various face amounts of insurance. As you suspect, however, as you grow older an insurance company takes greater risk insuring your life.

A renewable term policy can be renewed every year or every 5, 10, 15, 20 years, or until a specific age, such as 65. The most common is annual renewable term. When your policy comes up for renewal each year, you have the right to renew the policy. However, your premium rises each time to compensate the insurance company for the extra risk it undertakes. Up to age 40 the increase is typically only a few cents per $1,000 coverage. However, the increase accelerates rapidly after your 40th birthday.

At each renewal date you have the option of lowering your level of coverage to keep your premiums down. However, you cannot raise your coverage without demonstrating that you are still insurable. This may only consist of completing a questionnaire or, if you are over 40, you most likely will be required to have a doctor's examination.

If you want to be sure that you can renew your policy each year, you can buy *guaranteed renewable* coverage. It will cost more than simple renewable, but you do not have to worry about losing your insurance coverage if your health deteriorates in the interim. For most practical purposes, term insurance after age 65 is too expensive to be of any real value for most people. Hopefully by then, your need for life insurance will be ended.

In discussing other types of insurance we have emphasized the importance of comparison shopping on a regular basis. This is particularly important with renewable term insurance. The pricing of term policies presents savvy consumers with the chance to save money.

Insurance companies have different sets of premiums for their term policies. The *current* is the published rate for first time-buyers. It is set low to entice new policyholders. The *guaranteed rate* is the maximum rate you would have to pay for a set period, usually five or ten years. The *renewal rate* is the rate at which you can renew your policy. The current rate is almost always much lower than the renewal rate, especially after a few years.

If you are still healthy, you can often save substantial money by switching policies and companies. For example, in 1988 a 40-year-old man in good health could buy term coverage at a rate of about 64 cents per $1,000. In two years that rate would rise to $1.44. That is about the same rate that a 52-year-old man would pay for first year coverage with that same company! Some companies restrict the ability to change policies. To get around that, go to a different company.

During the term of coverage, your hope is that the insurance company is well-managed and in control of its expenses. That way you won't get bumped up to the guaranteed rate (the highest of the three rates). At the time you purchase the policy you know how much you will pay while the current-rate applies and the maximum you may have to pay after the current rate ends. The key is to buy a policy with a long current-rate schedule from a well-run, profitable insurance company.

When evaluating a term policy, look at the total premium for the length of time you expect to keep the policy. For example, if you need coverage for ten years, don't make a buying decision based on what the first year's premium will be. Look at what the premium costs will be over the full ten-year period. Companies' rate schedules vary widely. Some start out very low but rise steeply thereafter. You may be able to avoid the hassle of changing policies every few years if you can find a competitive premium schedule over five or ten years.

Your life insurance agent may want to sell you flat premium term for five or ten years. This simply means that the premium stays the same for the term of the insurance. However, you are not getting something for nothing. Basically what happens is that you pay more for coverage in the first few years of the policy than you otherwise would. You must decide whether that is a wise expenditure or whether you could put that money to better use elsewhere.

Other Types of Term Policies

Decreasing term has a benefit value that gets smaller every month or year while the premium stays the same. Typically, decreasing term is sold as a one-year renewable policy. Your premium stays constant as the protection level declines as you grow older.

Most company group life plans are for *level term to age 65*. This type of insurance provides the same protection at a constant premium year in and year out. It is the longest term of unrenewed protection of any term policy. As you would expect, premiums are higher in the early years than most renewable policies, but lower later.

Mortgage term insurance is a form of decreasing term. However, it decreases in uneven amounts, keeping pace with the reduction of the principal balance due on your mortgage loan. In the early years, when most of your mortgage dollars go to paying interest, mortgage term coverage declines slowly. Later though, when your mortgage payments start paying down principal, your mortgage term coverage declines much quicker.

This is generally relatively expensive coverage. If what you want is to pay off your mortgage (not always a good idea if you have a low-interest loan), buying term insurance with adequate limits may be smarter. Be sure to compare prices with other types of coverage before buying this coverage.

Deposit term insurance is a bit of a misnomer. It is not really term insurance because it has a savings element. You pay a premium each year. However, during the first year of coverage you pay an extra premium which is called a *deposit*. At the end of the coverage period, usually ten years, you may get back double the extra premium paid in the first year. What you have actually done is helped the company pay its salesperson's commission that first year. When you get back double the amount in ten years, you haven't really had savings as much as you are getting a rebate for overpaying your premiums. We don't recommend that you pay more for basic protection than is necessary, regardless of how cleverly designed the program may be!

Cash Value Insurance

Cash value insurance provides both death protection and a savings feature (the cash value of a policy after a set period of time). A portion of the annual premium goes to pay for the death protection, and the balance goes into savings that build up the cash value of the policy. At age 25, approximately 70 percent of the premiums in the initial years go into the savings component. Over the first 20 years about 40 to 50 percent of the premiums build up as savings. After a set period, an insured will get the accumulated cash value if the policy is terminated. *Only the face amount is paid if you die, no matter what the level of cash value at the time.*

A cash value policy is nothing more than a decreasing term policy and a savings plan put together. As your investment increases, your protection decreases. The gain in the savings element offsets the loss in the protection component, so the face amount stays the same. It may seem confusing when we say that your protection decreases if the face amount of the policy stays the same. But remember, you have put more and more of your own money into the fixed face amount of coverage (the savings element) that will be paid to your beneficiary. It is as though you have been putting money into a savings account. Upon your death, that savings account (minus sometimes substantial administrative fees assessed by the insurance company) is turned over to your beneficiary.

Many companies have a provision in their policies which gives them the right to wait six months to let you have your cash surrender value if you decide to drop the policy. Or they may make a loan to you on your *own* money (the cash value) for a preset period. They may not always insist on applying the provision, but you should know if it is there before making any buying decision.

A major sales point that insurance companies push about cash value is that you can borrow against the cash value. Until recently, there were tax advantages to being able to borrow against a cash value policy. However, we have yet to understand the attraction of paying interest (even "below market rate" as many companies used to advertise) to borrow your own money! The more recent trend toward variable rates on borrowings from cash value insurance certainly limits the appeal of this feature even further.

There are three basic kinds of cash value insurance and two types of hybrid policies:

Ordinary, whole life, and straight life are different names for the same policy. The premiums are set at the age when you buy the policy and remain level throughout your lifetime, or until you cash in the policy. Ordinary life's structure has changed little since the 19th century.

Your premium goes to pay for your death protection, the insurance company's expenses (including commissions), and the balance to a savings account. Your savings account earns interest at a rate set by the insurance company. That rate is typically below what you could earn outside an insurance policy.

A form of ordinary life called *participating whole life* is offered by mutual insurance companies. With a mutual company, policyholders are also the company's legal owners. If your mutual insurer is well-run or lucky in experiencing fewer claims than it expected, you will receive *dividends*. These are paid in addition to the fixed (usually low) interest rate paid on the savings portion of your policy. Dividends are essentially a refund of premium overcharges. In the 1960s and 1970s, dividend rates were quite low. However, in the 1980s pushed by competitive forces, dividend rates have edged higher to as much as 7 percent or 8 percent. Of course, the problem is that there are no guarantees that these higher rates will stay around.

Limited payment life is similar to ordinary life but is paid up at a certain point before age 65. It then stays in force after that. The idea is that the premiums will be paid during your highest income years. However, this is not always a blessing. Young families with children and a mortgage are often hard-pressed to stretch their income as it is to pay for basic necessities.

Premium payments remain level to the point they cease. The insurance company is able to maintain coverage once premium payments have stopped because the premiums charged are higher than what you would pay for comparable ordinary life coverage. The shorter the premium period (typical periods are 10 years, 20 years, and to age 65), the higher the premiums and the faster the cash buildup. These policies have declined in popularity as other heavily marketed hybrid policies have moved to the fore. They are rarely sold anymore.

Endowment policies build up cash value so that the death benefit is entirely covered by the cash you have paid in. Policies are written with maturities of 10, 20, or 30 years or to age 60, 65, or 70. They are designed to build up an investment while being protected. However, at maturity there is no protection left. Endowment policies mature within a certain number of years. You can receive your own money back (what a deal!) while still living. Another way to think of it is as piggybank insurance. Few endowment policies are written any more.

Hybrid policies combine features of both term and cash value insurance. The first widely accepted hybrid life policy was *universal life* introduced in 1980. Only two years later, universal life accounted for 12 percent of all life insurance premium payments. Most of that growth came at the expense of ordinary life, which had been paying a lowly 3 or 4 percent on the savings element.

Universal Life Insurance

Originally called *flexible-premium adjustable life,* universal life features an adjustable interest rate to be paid on the savings portion of your policy. That contrasts with the fixed rate paid by ordinary life. As you may have guessed from the original name, the interest rate paid on the cash value is not the only thing which can fluctuate. You can vary the premiums you pay. In fact, rather than calling these payment premiums, universal policies refer to them as *contributions.* For example, you may want to spend more money when interest rates being paid on the savings are high. And assuming you have sufficient cash value built up in the policy, you can even skip payments if you are short of cash.

However, it is important for the continuity of your coverage to be sure that your accumulated cash value is enough to make the payments for death protection and the company's fees. You receive regular statements that detail the amount of cash you have accumulated. Typically, the cash value of your policy is assessed a monthly fee for death protection and expenses. Unlike ordinary life, these assessments are spelled out in detail for you. You must be careful not to skip too many payments though, because if the monthly charges eat up your cash value, the policy may lapse leaving your family without coverage.

One distinguishing feature of universal life is the variable interest rate that the company pays on the savings portion of the policy. This rate is usually set at specific intervals by the insurance company or is tied to some sort of index. Basically this allows the insurance company to shift the investment risk to you, since the minimum guaranteed rate is usually very low (3 percent or 4 percent). With its lower risk, it can afford to charge lower premiums. For example, the annual premium for $100,000 of coverage for a man at age 35 can be about 50 percent of the premium charged for ordinary life.

As a result, universal life is often sold as the cash-value alternative for younger buyers who cannot afford ordinary life. However, that assumes that some type of cash-value insurance is better than term. That is a questionable assumption at best.

The big attraction to universal life, especially when it was first introduced, was the high advertised interest rates being paid on the savings portion of policies. However, the returns are subject to many restrictions. For example, to get a certain return you must leave the money in for a set period of time (typically three or four years) or the return on the first $1,000 of accumulated cash value is less than on amounts above that. And don't forget the front-end "load charges" (commissions) that come off the top of each contribution.

If there is enough cash buildup in your policy, you may decide whether to allocate part of that money to pay the policy premium. Generally if you "borrow" in this way from the policy's cash value, you will not be charged interest and your death benefits will not be reduced. That also contrasts with ordinary life where loans are charged a set interest rate, and unpaid loans are deducted from the death benefits payable upon the policyholder's death.

Depending on the interest the company is able to get on its investments (which it has to tell you), your premium may cost nothing, though you may have to contribute something to build up the cash value.

The cash buildup in these policies is tax-deferred. However, the federal government has moved to tighten tax rules relating to cash value insurance policies. Most likely, the ability to borrow against your cash value, tax-free, will be changed in the not-too-distant future. In October 1988, Congress eliminated the ability of policyholders of single-premium life policies to borrow against their policies tax-free.

While universal life is better than ordinary life in terms of the potential cash value growth, it is probably not as good as buying term insurance and investing the difference on your own. We will get into that in more detail shortly.

Variable Life Insurance

Variable life is similar to universal life. Like universal life, it has two distinct elements: death protection and variable savings. The death benefit is covered by term insurance, which is paid by a portion of your premium. However, the savings portion is not tied to a fixed-income investment. The cash buildup is dependent on the performance of the money invested in stocks or bonds, typically through mutual funds.

Depending on which investments you want your funds to be invested in, the cash value of your policy can vary widely. Imagine having your savings invested in stocks in 1986 and up to August 1987. Your return would have far outdistanced a universal policy tied to short-term interest rates. However, think back to stock market performance following the August 1987 peak. A thunderous recordbreaking crash occurred a few short months later in October.

Variable life is sold through a prospectus that assures you of the most complete disclosure of fees, terms, and performance histories of all life policies. Unlike universal life, the investment performance can affect not only your cash value but your death benefit as well. While there is a guaranteed death benefit, it is far costlier than either universal or ordinary life, and of course, term.

Obviously the attraction of variable life is all on the investment side. It doesn't make much sense to plan on a specific amount of necessary death protection, and then to gamble it away by buying a variable policy that can reduce the death benefit to the minimum guaranteed level if your selected investment markets go into a headlong slide. After all, your dependents' needs are unlikely to vary with the fate of the markets.

The strongest marketing for variable life policies has been focused on the fact that your cash value grows on a tax-deferred basis as long as you do not withdraw any of your investment earnings. As mentioned above, you can borrow against your cash value, but Congress is looking very closely at taking away tax benefits for life insurance products.

Don't be fooled by very attractive sounding sales pitches on the high returns available with variable life policies. Where there is the possibility of high returns there is also the chance of very poor returns. Also, fees tend to be very high with these policies. Monitor management fees and be aware of early withdrawal penalties.

Deciding Which to Buy: Term or Cash Value?

The question of whether cash value or term insurance is the best way to go to meet your protection needs requires you to answer two questions:

1. How long do you need the coverage?
2. What yield can you earn on your investments?

If your projected need for insurance is fewer than 12 years, term insurance is probably the better buy. It takes at least ten years and sometimes longer for the cash value of your policy to equal your total investment. Only after that initial accumulation period can the policy's value begin to grow beyond your investment. Similarly, if you can earn a consistently good rate of return with the premium money you save in the early years of coverage by purchasing term rather than cash value insurance, it is even more likely that term insurance will be less expensive than whole life insurance.

Table 6-2 compares a $100,000 Occidental Life Trendsetter Annual Renewable Term policy with an Assured Life *interest-sensitive* Whole Life Policy, assuming an interest rate of 11 percent. It also assumes that the difference in premiums between the policies can be invested at 9 percent after taxes. If you watch the growth of the "Difference at 9 percent" column and compare it to the "Cash Value" column, you will notice that the two begin to break even between years 12 and 13.

In other words, if you can invest the difference between the term rate (Trendsetter) and the whole life rate (Assured Life) consistently at 9 percent per year (after tax) *and* your need for life insurance is for 13 years or fewer, you should buy term insurance. If your need is for 13 years or longer *or* you couldn't achieve a 9 percent yield, you should choose the whole life alternative.

Comparing Policies

When you are seeking a life insurance policy, don't make the mistake of buying the company rather than the policy. Make sure that the policy is exactly what you need. Often the same company offers relatively similar policies at widely different prices. Don't be conned into buying a policy because a salesperson can point to an independent survey that rates a company's product highly, only to find out you were sold the high-priced version!

By the same token, you don't want to buy a policy from a company that is liable to go under at any moment. If you have a cash value policy, you may lose all your accumulated savings. All life insurance companies are rated annually by A.M. Best & Company. You can find the latest issue of *Best's Insurance Reports* in most libraries. Stick with companies rated A or A + .

Comparing the many different life insurance policies is a trying task for a full-time professional, to say nothing of an average consumer. The National Insurance Consumer Organization (121 North Payne Street, Alexandria, VA 22314) offers different publications to help consumers sort through the complexities and hyperbole of insurance advertising claims. Their booklet, "Taking the Bite Out of Insurance," features a list of the maximum rates they recommend paying for renewable term policies.

By now you may have concluded that it would take a full-time staff of consultants just to compare the relative merits of the many different insurance policies. Realizing that the average consumer is simply not equipped to compare even cash value to cash value policies, the National Association of Insurance Commissioners has developed two indexes that give you single numbers for

TABLE 6–2
Net Premium Schedule for Comparing Term and Whole Life Policies

Year	Trendsetter Premium	Assured Life	Difference	Difference at 9%	Cash Value Assuming 11% Interest Rate
1	145	561	416	453	0
2	159	561	402	932	0
3	175	561	386	1,436	0
4	193	561	368	1,966	206
5	212	561	349	2,523	712
6	288	561	273	3,047	1,276
7	304	561	257	3,601	1,890
8	325	561	236	4,182	2,649
9	350	561	211	4,788	3,382
10	380	561	181	5,416	4,285
11	414	0	(414)	5,452	4,687
12	449	0	(449)	5,453	5,212
13	489	0	(489)	5,410	5,662
14	532	0	(532)	5,317	6,216
15	581	0	(581)	5,162	6,686
16	636	0	(636)	4,933	7,175
17	696	0	(696)	4,618	7,673
18	764	0	(764)	4,200	8,182
19	840	0	(840)	3,662	8,704
20	925	0	(925)	2,983	9,239
Total	8,857	5,610			

comparing similar policies. The indexes won't tell you whether a term policy is better than an ordinary life policy. However, they are good guides for comparing policies of the same type. You will need to go through the exercise we outlined above to choose between term and cash value.

The indexes' greatest value is in helping you choose between different policies of the same type but with varying premiums and cash values. For example, should you select an ordinary life policy with a low annual premium but also low cash values, or is the better choice a whole life participating policy that charges more for the same death benefit but projects greater cash values?

The *interest-adjusted net payment cost indexes* come in two varieties: the *surrender cost index* and the *net payment cost index*. The net payment cost index measures the present value of the premiums you pay for the next 10 years. The index factors in the interest you could be earning on your premium dollars. The important thing to remember when using the interest-adjusted net payment cost index is that the higher the index number, the higher the cost for $1,000 of insurance protection. All other things being equal, you would want the policy with the lowest index number. Watch the net payment cost index most closely if you expect to hold your policy beyond 10 years.

The surrender cost index measures the present cost of cash value policies if you cancel them to take your cash in 10 years. As with the net payment cost index, what you are looking for is the lowest number consonant with your other requirements. The surrender cost index is the one you should watch particularly closely if you anticipate cashing in your policy.

Most state regulators require insurance agents to provide these numbers on request. If the agent is reluctant or slow to produce these numbers, you should look elsewhere. The policy he or she is pushing is probably a high-cost item.

If you want to do your own homework rather than entertaining a number of life insurance salespeople, you can find a concise listing of the net cost index numbers in A. M. Best Company's monthly *Best's Review*.

However, as we mentioned above, do not try to use the index to compare the cost of term insurance to cash value. The cash value will always appear cheaper because the cash value policy is actually providing less "pure" death protection as time passes.

When using the interest adjusted net-cost indexes, you should also be careful that you are comparing similar policies. Different riders can affect premiums substantially. For example, a guaranteed renewable rider will cause the premium to be higher.

One last alternative you may want to consider is to pay someone else to do all that comparison shopping homework. A number of "rate-screening services" have sprung up in recent years that will screen term policies to match your personal profile and desired amount of coverage with companies offering competitive rates. They usually charge a fee, or take a commission if they match you up with what you need.

Typically, you give the service information about yourself. The company then sends you a printout of 5 to 10 companies with their annual term rates for periods of as much as 20 years in the future. One company that sells only the screening service and not insurance is Insurance Information Inc., of Methuan, Mass., (800)472-5800. They monitor over 200 companies and charge $50 to send you the names and rates of five low-cost insurance companies that meet your requirements.

Insurance as an Investment

Following the passage of the Tax Reform Act of 1986 which eliminated many tax-shelter investments, the insurance industry launched an aggressive campaign to sell single-premium variable life insurance as one of the few remaining legitimate tax sheltered investments. Touted as an investment that earns a higher tax-free return than municipal bonds while including "free insurance," single-premium whole life insurance sounded like the perfect answer to many people's investment questions. Sales boomed to $9.4 billion in 1987.

Single-premium life insurance policies are mostly investment products combined with a little bit of insurance to give them their tax-deferral status. As you no doubt inferred, with these policies you pay the premium only once. Premiums range from $50,000 to $1 million or more. For that investment, you get a paid-up insurance policy (the death benefit depends on your age and can change depending on whether you borrow from the policy). In addition, you get an investment account that can earn money on a tax-deferred basis so long as you do not cash out the policy. In that case, you must pay taxes on the earnings.

Generally, single-premium policies quote a *net* (yield after deducting insurance and administrative fees) interest rate that is earned by your cash value. You pay for the insurance each year, much the same way a universal life policy provides for payment. It is taken out of the buildup in your cash value.

If you are looking primarily for protection, you will be puzzled by the sales pitches for this product. Rarely is the death benefit mentioned. Rather it is sold for its tax benefits. Your earnings within the policy accumulate tax-free, just like an IRA account. And just like an IRA account, if you cash it in early, you will be taxed on everything earned while inside the cover of the policy.

Up until June 1988 though, you could get around that by simply borrowing against your policy. However, Congress moved to close that loophole retroactive to June when it passed a tax technical correction bill in October 1988. The tax bill eliminated the ability to take tax-free loans from single-premium life policies purchased after June 21, 1988.

Money taken out before age 59.5 is subject to a 10 percent penalty tax as well as ordinary income tax on the gains. Single-premium life insurance maintained other tax advantages including tax-deferral on investment gains and tax-free payment of death benefits to beneficiaries.

While changes in the tax law should temper some of the more blatant investment-oriented sales of life insurance, you will likely still run into this pitch. As we have said before, if what you are looking for is the protection that life insurance provides for your family, then you are better off simply buying that protection, usually in the form of term insurance, and investing the balance.

The large initial investment required for single-premium life policies limits your flexibility to pursue other good investments. And finally, insurance companies do not provide their services as a public service. They make money by assessing fees for the administrative tasks involved in running the programs. Some fees to watch out for include surrender (or withdrawal) charges that are assessed if you terminate the policy early (usually in the first seven years). Others include front-end charges, annual administrative fees, a premium tax in some states, an annual one percent "mortality and risk-expense guarantee" fee, and management fees for running the investment funds. Usually the management fees and expenses of no-load mutual funds are lower than the equivalent fees for insurance company funds.

Watching Out for Those Contract Clauses

Most insurance contracts have eight main clauses that are much more than mere window dressing. Each of these clauses involves important decisions you must make in determining which can aid you in achieving your goals. Choosing the right contract is as personal as choosing the people you live with. You must understand the clauses well to know what protection you are getting for your loved ones.

The *beneficiary clause* spells out two classes of beneficiaries. The *primary beneficiary* is the person designated by the insured to receive your death benefits. If the primary beneficiary dies before the policy's proceeds are completely paid out, the *contingent beneficiaries* will receive the remainder of the policy's benefits. For example, it is common for a spouse to be named primary beneficiary. However, if both the insured and the spouse die in an accident, contingent beneficiaries such as their children have not been named, the proceeds could get wrapped up in legal wrangling. That wouldn't do anybody any good except perhaps some attorneys who will collect their fees to straighten things out eventually.

The *loan clause* describes when and how you can borrow on the savings buildup in your cash value policy. In case of your death, the face amount will usually be reduced by the amount of the loan if it is not repaid. Typically, the interest rate charged is less than the rates you could get elsewhere. There are usually no fees or carrying charges imposed. You can repay the loan at your convenience or not at all. It all sounds very attractive until you realize that you are paying to borrow your own money.

The *premium payment clause* stipulates how you are to pay your premiums. Normally, premiums are paid annually, though you can also choose semiannual or some other method. The least expensive method is to pay annually, since most companies assess additional fees if you elect some other way. These extra fees can be quite substantial if you want to pay monthly or quarterly.

The *dividend clause* spells out the details of the dividend policy. This is most significant in participating life insurance policies where the dividends are heavily used as a marketing tool. As we discussed above, these "dividends" are not the same as the dividends that publicly owned stock companies pay out of earnings to their stockholders. Dividends in life insurance policies are really rebates of premium overcharges by *mutual companies* (those companies legally owned by their policyholders). When a mutual company pays dividends it means that it had overestimated the number and amount of claims it would face during the year. So it passes the "savings" on to the policyholders as a dividend.

On the other hand, stock companies pay a real dividend to their stockholders when they've made a profit. They also offer participating (par) policies to their insureds. These par policies also pay a dividend that comes from intentionally overcharged premiums. That is why they have the funds available to make the payments!

There are six different dividend options available if you buy a participating policy in either a mutual or a stock company. You can:

1. spend it;
2. apply it to your premium payments;
3. leave it with the company to draw interest;
4. use it for paid-up cash value additions (buy additional coverage in the form of single-premium policies);
5. buy a paid-up term policy and get much more protection than with cash value additions but no "savings"; or
6. use some to buy a term policy and leave the balance with the company to earn interest.

The *nonforfeiture clause* defines what the company will do if you default on your cash value policy. You have three options to choose from:

1. withdraw the cash value (*the cash surrender value*) in a lump sum;
2. trade the cash value for a smaller, face value, paid-up policy; or

3. trade it for a paid-up term policy of a shorter period with the same face amount.

If you fail to make a choice and you discontinue your policy, the third option is automatically selected for you. The details of these options are printed in tables on the policy.

The *reinstatement clause* allows policyholders whose policies have lapsed or been discontinued to put them in force again if 1) they have not already redeemed the cash surrender value; 2) they pay all owed premiums plus interest; and 3) they request reinstatement within a set time after discontinuance.

The *change of policy clause* allows you to change to a different policy with different coverage. For example, if you have a ten-year guaranteed renewable term policy, you may want to convert it to a variable life cash value policy. Since the cash value or whole life policy will be substantially more expensive, the company will charge you the difference in premiums plus a carrying charge. With all the different types of policies and with your changing life circumstances, it would not be unusual to want to change. Be sure to check out the price differences with not only your present insurer but with competitors of the new policy you need.

The *suicide prevention clause* states that no benefits will be paid if the policyholder commits suicide within two years of the policy's purchase date.

Customizing the Policy to Fit Your Needs

In addition to the different clauses we have delineated above, you have further options to tailor your policy to suit your particular needs. One reason why we recommend finding a responsible, conscientious agent is that after working with you for awhile, he or she will be able to anticipate your needs and recommend the additional touches that make a difference.

A policy *rider* is a specialized provision that is added to a policy for a specific purpose. Typical policy options and riders (which usually come at an extra cost) include:

1. The *renewability* option allows you to renew the policy without a medical examination. This rider does not change the fact, though, that your premiums may be higher for each subsequent period.

2. The *convertibility* option allows you to exchange one kind of insurance for another without a medical examination. The face amount coverage of your new policy may, however, be limited.

3. The *guaranteed insurability rider* allows you to increase the face amount of the policy by specific amounts at specific dates without a medical examination. You may want to consider this if you anticipate increasing insurance protection needs.

4. The *disability of waiver* option says that if you become disabled the insurance company will keep your coverage intact. Normally there is a six-month waiting period after the beginning of your disability period.

5. The *cost-of-living adjustment rider* automatically increases the face amount of your policy. Your premium will also increase to reflect the higher coverage. If you reject a cost-of-living adjustment you may forfeit your right to future cost-of-living adjustments in your policy.

6. The *accidental death benefit* option states that if your death is due to an accident (as opposed to an illness) the death benefit will be some multiple (e.g., two or three times) the face amount of the policy. The most common provision is double indemnity, a doubling of the face amount.

There are other options and riders too numerous to spell out in detail here. But you should get the point. If you have a particular need, ask your agent. You never know, there may be a special provision that will fit your situation exactly.

Settlement Options

And just when you thought your decision-making was complete, you are confronted with one final round of choices: settlement options. When you buy your life insurance policy you have the privilege of deciding how death benefits will be distributed to your beneficiaries. Of course, if you are still kicking when the policy matures, you can choose how you should be paid!

There are four primary options:

1. The *installment option* pays you or your beneficiary installments in whatever fixed amounts you want until all the benefits are distributed. Or this option allows for equal installments being paid out over a specified period of time.

The interest rate paid on the balance is usually guaranteed at a very low rate. If you die after collecting on your matured policy before the benefits are exhausted, your beneficiaries get the remaining balance.

The advantage of installment payments is that you spread the taxable gain over a period of years. That advantage is lost when payments are made to a beneficiary, though, since life insurance proceeds are not subject to income tax.

2. The *interest option* is for withdrawing interest income only. In this case, you leave the proceeds with the company and draw only the interest on an annual, semiannual, quarterly, or monthly basis. You retain ownership of the entire cash value of your policy. It becomes part of your estate when you die. This option may be changed at will. You may elect to receive a lump-sum payment at any time.

3. The *life annuity option* pays benefits to the beneficiary (or policy-holder in the case of a policy which has matured) for as long as he or she lives. There are four different types of *standard annuity options*

Straight life annuity offers payments to the policyholder forever. This is a good deal if you live long enough to collect more than was put in, plus interest. However, for this to pay off, you must outlive the normal life expectancy by 10 to 25 years to beat the odds. The drawback is if you don't beat the odds. If you (or more likely your beneficiary) die prematurely, the company keeps everything that is left.

A *refund annuity* makes payments during the policyholder's lifetime. It pays beneficiaries upon his or her death. Since the company must eventually pay back the entire investment, the minimum guaranteed payment rate is lower than for a straight life annuity. You might choose this option if you had reason to believe you weren't going to live long or if you wanted to leave an estate to your heirs. Usually though, in either of these cases, you would be better off investing on your own rather than tying up your money in an annuity.

Certain and continuous annuity also pays for life. If the insured dies within a specified period (usually 5, 10, or 20 years) payments are made to beneficiaries for the remainder of the period. There *may* be some reason, somewhere, somehow, for choosing this kind of settlement. It just escapes us for the moment!

Joint and survivorship annuity offers lifetime income for two people (who do not need to be related) even if one outlives the other. If one dies, the second receives the payments at either the same amount, two-thirds, or one-half the amount paid to both people. The smaller the payment chosen for the second person alone, the larger the payment will be beforehand for them together. There is a guaranteed minimum rate the company must pay, regardless of its investment returns.

4. The *lump sum option* is self-explanatory. You or your beneficiary take the face amount of the policy in a single lump-sum.

Assuming your beneficiaries prefer to steer their own courses, the lump-sum payment option is certainly the best alternative. The money can be put into higher paying investment vehicles than the insurance company is likely to offer. That means that the initial amount you need for the policy's face amount can be lowered. That, of course, would save on insurance premiums from the beginning.

For example, if the beneficiary needs $3,000 a year in supplemental income, that money can be gained from only a $30,000 investment in a savings certificate paying 10 percent. But if your insurance policy pays only 3 percent, you would have to have $100,000 face amount just to produce the same amount of income.

If your concern is that your beneficiaries will spend the whole amount quickly and frivolously, you might consider setting up a trust fund for them. After all, a wild and crazy spending blowout would defeat the whole purpose of your careful planning in selecting and buying the proper coverage to meet the needs of your dependents. You might designate a banker or lawyer to invest the funds and distribute the proceeds as you specify.

The settlement option you select may be the most important decision you make in terms of providing adequate coverage at the cheapest cost. For most situations, we feel that the lump-sum option is the only sensible choice.

Consider the difference in proceeds between low-risk and high-risk investing. No matter what the choice is along the risk scale, your beneficiaries can *nearly always* get higher yields doing their own investing than they would get by leaving any part of the money with an insurance company. The insurance company's fees alone will reduce their return substantially.

The Need for Comparison Shopping

When looking for the right life insurance policy you need to stay lean and mean. Ask questions and demand good, clear answers. Now that there are so many more participants in the insurance business (e.g., full-service stockbrokers now sell insurance) changes now occur very rapidly. You must be kept up to date to be properly protected without being premium poor. That job is your agent's responsibility.

Your best bet may be an independent agent who represents several companies. He or she may then have more loyalty to you than to any given company. The more an agent knows, the more he or she can tell you. Check out the agent's education and certifications just as you would a medical specialist.

The relationship with your agent is a key factor in being sure that you have the protection you need at the right price. Don't settle for the first salesperson who knocks on your door. A little time spent interviewing prospective agents will pay dividends for years to come.

WRAPPING UP

The purpose of life insurance is financial protection for your dependents in the event of your untimely death. While the advertising claims of many insurers push the investment or tax advantages of life insurance, your interest should be in what kind of protection your life insurance policy will provide at what price.

While admittedly it is easier said than done, it is important to set aside your emotions and turn to the calculator for most life insurance questions. What you need and what price to pay are logical questions that can be best answered with a look at the appropriate math.

Life insurance and investments are not for the same purpose. They rarely make the most profitable combination. Banking with your insurance company or buying a participating policy is usually not the best use of your insurance dollars.

You now have a good understanding of life insurance, and certainly know where to look for clarification if you are troubled by further questions about contract clauses, options, and riders. First and foremost make sure your policy is renewable under terms you can afford as long as you will need it.

Now that you know that life insurance is really death insurance, it is unlikely that you will be easily misled by all the other reasons that are often advanced to convince you to buy it. It is equally likely, that thus forearmed, you will get the most for your premium dollar because you know what you really need from it.

We believe that annual renewable term insurance offers the best coverage at the best price for most people. The most satisfying way to beat the life insurance game is to pay the premiums while you need the coverage. Then live a long and fulfilling life.

CHAPTER 7

END PAPER

WHO ARE YOU?

At this point you understand the key elements of good insurance coverage. However, emotions often get in the way of reason. For many of you, the actual process of buying coverage will present a conflict between your psychological makeup and the cold, calculating logic of our many examples. What is most important is that you acquire the insurance coverage that provides the peace of mind you need to pursue your dreams (we doubt that evaluating and buying insurance plays a very big part in most people's dreams!).

In the following pages we have included questionnaires that are designed to help you understand your motives more clearly. By identifying some of the very issues that insurance companies use as ammunition in selling policies, rather than serving needs, you will be ahead of the game.

Slaying Your Emotional Dragons

Consider your financial protection in the face of the unknown. It can be scary! However, you can increase your ability to control the "what if" demons in your life. Start by recognizing that you and you alone occupy the primary seat of power unless you choose to leave it vacant for someone else to take command. And that is exactly what happens if you neglect your insurance needs. If you have an accident or loss that is not covered by insurance, someone else is determining your financial future. Now that is scary!

We've all experienced the there-is-nothing-I-can-do feeling. Sometimes we harbor that helpless feeling too long, leaving ourselves very vulnerable.

The majority of this book has been designed to help you understand the facts of insurance. The following exercises will help you develop the skills and the confidence to plan as you go, rather than wishing you had done so after the fact. In other words, by doing something for yourself that is your responsibility anyway, you will feel that sense of helplessness slide away like water from a duck's back. Think of life with reduced stress. That feeling should help motivate you to finally tackle your insurance needs and get that chore out of the way!

The Bottom Line

The bottom line of what you learn in this book can be summed up in one word—*results*. And, do you know what? This may be the only game in town where you can be sure of the score before the game is over. You will never have to hang your head afterward and cry, "If only I had done something."

Understanding is the key. Hopefully, by the time you have reached this point (if you are not one of those who turn first to the back of a book!), you know that comprehending the world of insurance is not as difficult as you may have thought. But it may very well be more important than you ever imagined.

Understanding insurance eliminates its myths and mysteries. It allows you to walk right by an agent's show-and-sell plan. It gives you the ability to take control of your own financial well-being.

What Are You?

Insurance is extremely personal. If you are not aware of who you are and your style of reacting to situations, such as your risk-taking and sales vulnerability temperament, it will be difficult to make intelligent decisions about protecting yourself financially.

Anyone who has gone through an introductory psychology course or has made it to adulthood should be familiar with the theory that men and women individually are greater than the sum of their parts.

Our identities—who we are—are an integration of thought and behavior. We are products of what we do as well as what we think. This is why it is important to know about yourself before making critical decisions about something as crucial as properly safeguarding your belongings and your family.

Actions Speak Louder

Ask yourself some probing questions, keeping in mind that we are made up of what we do, not just what we think. For example, say you bump into a colleague from a previous job whom you haven't seen for many months, and you insist that you "get together for lunch soon." But then you never call the person. Something is out of whack with either your sense of follow-through or your sincerity. Your thinking and actions are contradictory. You are presenting a dishonest picture to others. You might begin to wonder why.

It is difficult to look objectively at yourself in order to define your decision-making tendencies to see how they connect with your thoughts and actions. Without help, it is at best confusing to attempt such an analysis.

First Things First

As a warmup exercise, see how you do in your own mind with the following situation:

You live alone in the rear ground-floor apartment in a four-unit building where rent is unbelievably cheap. You have use of a small but very nice garden right outside the kitchen. You love the place and it seems perfect for your lifestyle right now. The problem is that the neighborhood crime rate has been steadily spiraling upward. Sometimes you think twice about going out or even coming home after dark because you have heard some bizarre stories of muggings—none first-hand, though.

As you step out of the shower, glad to have the chance to get to bed early for a change, you hear a strange noise at your bedroom window. You know that you are the only one home in the building because there were no lights on when you got home. You hear another noise. It certainly is not a bird or squirrel at this hour. If it is a mouse, it sounds like it uses a screwdriver. You have to think of your alternatives and make a decision. Fast!!

Do you:

1. hide in the closet and pray, hoping it is all a bad dream?
2. grab your target pistol and shoot the window out?
3. go out to the garden and tackle the intruder from behind?
4. quietly call the police and run out the front door screaming?
5. scream loudly, snatch your robe and piggy bank and get out any way you can?

As you ponder some of these choices, and maybe add a few of your own, you are beginning to think in terms of how you cope under stressful conditions (actively or passively); how you see the means to a given end (calmly or overwhelmingly); whether you are impulsive or practical; and how much you value controlling a situation.

To be more specific, if you were burglarized would your inclination be to move out immediately or to stay and install an alarm system? This question should also serve to trigger your thinking about your renter's or real property coverage, your personal property, health and disability, or even life insurance coverage. Are they adequate?

Write It Down

It is said that the greatest force the written word can exercise is its ability to inflame one's mind, one's heart, one's conscience into action—good or bad—without raising public embarrassment.

It is important for you to discover your insurance control-taking style. By answering the questions in the "Taking Stock, Your Control-Taking Style" worksheet that follows, you will get a better understanding of your general insurance-slanted profile in the broad picture of who you are.

You can't know who you are until you see what you say. There is usually something in between what we say out loud, or even to ourselves, and what we mean. Writing it down often provides the missing link. You may be surprised.

Your Control-Taking Personality

We can never really be prepared for changes, even if we are positive enough to insist that starting over is what keeps life fresh. We always have to adjust, and a radical adjustment can severely rattle our self-esteem.

Personality is a compound balance of many conflicting forces, tensions, diversions, and demands that somehow tends to stay its course and shape our behavior unless something happens from without or within to change it. In healthy people there is always a choice within the bounds of their personalities to say yes, no, or maybe to everything.

Saying nothing is making a choice, so you can never really say accurately, "I had no choice," unless you are victimized by an accident. But even then, you could have shaped an excellent estate plan and still have been in control of directing what is left. You always have a choice if you take the time to be aware and to think and act. Of course, your choices are not necessarily entirely rational. Your biases and fears and personal demons will lean heavily as each question arises.

The following Taking Stock questionnaire is not a test. It is merely a tool to help you comprehend your decision-making behavior as it applies to protecting what is yours. It provides a brief look at your style of controlling problem situations and your tough-to-tender inclinations (vulnerability).

Insight is the merging of experience, knowledge, and intuition. Each of these factors affects every decision you make every day. Understanding your control-taking style gives you the opportunity to accept it as it is or to make a conscious decision to change your behavior and take a more rational stance. By doing this you will gain better control over your life.

| **Taking Stock** |

Your Control-Taking Style

Several different reactions (solutions) are suggested for each of the problems given below. You should circle either Agree or Disagree for *each* option, (a) through (d), to indicate whether you think that solution is one you would use or agree with, or the opposite. Don't think about your answer a long time or try to analyze it. Just use your gut reaction. When you have finished this questionnaire, turn to the evaluation that follows for instructions on how to score and interpret your answers.

Here is a sample exercise:

If the weather forecast showed a 60% chance of rain, I would probably

a. stay home and turn on the TV.   Agree (Disagree)

b. take an umbrella when I went out.   (Agree) Disagree

c. ignore the forecast; it's usually wrong.   Agree (Disagree)

d. do nothing now; worry about it later   Agree (Disagree)

In the preceding sample the person thought choice (b) would be an agreeable solution in most cases and that choices (a), (c), and (d) would rarely be agreeable solutions. In each of the problem situations that follow, you may agree with all of the solutions, some of them, or none of them. It is important that you circle one alternative for each choice as we demonstrated above.

---

1. If there were an earthquake or flood near where I lived and worked, and the newspaper made wild predictions about the future, I would probably

    a. call insurance companies about special coverage rates.   **Agree   Disagree**

    b. ignore it and go about my business.   **Agree   Disagree**

    c. ask for a job transfer to a safer place.   **Agree   Disagree**

    d. worry more, but do nothing.   **Agree   Disagree**

---

2. If I had all the insurance protection I needed for the next ten years, I would probably

    a. still check with my agent every year or so to make certain I was well covered.   **Agree   Disagree**

    b. feel I had accomplished something, and rest easy.   **Agree   Disagree**

Your Control-Taking Style *(continued)*

    c. listen carefully if I heard of a new kind of policy.   **Agree** **Disagree**
    d. depend on my agent to alert me to a new coverage.   **Agree** **Disagree**

3. If I had only one month to live, I would

    a. get my affairs in order.   **Agree** **Disagree**

    b. be immobilized by depression.   **Agree** **Disagree**

    c. do something I had always secretly wanted to do.   **Agree** **Disagree**

    d. depend on my family and friends for help.   **Agree** **Disagree**

4. My life is the way it is because of

    a. decisions I have made along the way.   **Agree** **Disagree**

    b. circumstances I had little control over.   **Agree** **Disagree**

    c. choices I would make all over again.   **Agree** **Disagree**

    d. the way my parents raised me.   **Agree** **Disagree**

5. I believe that

    a. each of us determine his/her own fate.   **Agree** **Disagree**

    b. luck plays a huge part in everyone's life.   **Agree** **Disagree**

    c. you work hard, live right, and get rewarded.   **Agree** **Disagree**

    d. timing is everything in life.   **Agree** **Disagree**

Your Vulnerability Quotient

In any kind of decision making, people are influenced not only by their active or passive control strategies, but also by how vulnerable they feel to loss. Some are sure that nothing bad will ever happen to them, and some are just as sure that something will. In either extreme case, overreaction is likely.

This section was devised to help you determine your vulnerability quotient. You are to *divide 100 points* among the 10 statements below, *depending on how much you agree with each of them*. If you agree equally with all statements, give each 10 points. If you agree with only 1, give that one 100 points and the rest 0. If you agree very strongly with 2 statements, somewhat with 2 others, and only a little with the remaining 6, you might assign 30 points to each that you agree with strongly, 17 points to ones you sort of agree with, and 1 point to each of the remaining statements. *Notice that the total of the points must equal 100.*

Your Control-Taking Style *(continued)*

---

1. I am a lucky person. _____

2. Nothing ventured, nothing gained. _____

3. I could lose everything I own, and it would not devastate me. _____

4. All's well that ends well. _____

5. Even when awful things happen to me, things turn out okay. _____

6. If you live long enough, trouble will find you. _____

7. When things go too well, I start to get nervous. _____

8. Into each life, a little rain must fall. _____

9. I am a careful person. _____

10. The conservative way is the best way. _____

Total Points   100

Evaluating Your Control-Taking Style

Determining Your Control-Taking Style

Some people control their lives and solve their problems by *doing* something. Anything. Some of their actions may be impulsive, may be foolish, or may even be destructive. They mistake motion for progress. Others take active control of their lives by carefully considering their options and basing their actions on educated decisions.

To determine your *active control score*, count how many times you agreed with the (a) and/or (c) alternatives in the first part of the exercise you just completed and enter your score here: _____

If you agreed with the (a) and/or (c) alternative 7 or more times, you tend to react to difficulties by applying *active control*. We expect that most people who buy this book either already, or will in the future, use active control in handling their lives, and would have a score of 5 or more.

Passive control is another way of solving problems. Essentially it is denying that a problem exists, turning to others for an answer, or hoping the problem will solve itself. To determine your passive control score, count up the number of times you chose the (b) and/or (d) alternative and enter your score here: _____

If you agreed with 7 or more statements, passive control is currently your behavior style. For instance, someone may have bought this book for you,

Your Control-Taking Style *(continued)*

rather than your having chosen to buy it yourself. If you agreed with 3 or fewer, passive control is not an important coping mechanism for you.

Determining Your Vulnerability Quotient

Add up the points you have assigned to statements 1 through 5 (tough you) and enter that score here:

Score A _____

Then add up the points you assigned to statements 6 through 10 (tender you) and enter that score here:

Score B _____

Now subtract your tough score (A) from your tender score (B), keeping in mind that if A is larger than B, you will have a minus figure. (20 − 80 = − 60). Look at the following chart to evaluate your quotient.

> **Score B** _____
> **Score A** − _____

Vulnerability Quotient _____

The way you protect yourself and what you have will be dictated by both your control-taking style and your feelings of vulnerability. The chart on page 116 takes both of these scores into account. Rather than complicating matters by boiling your scores down to one figure and pegging yourself to a specific spot, simply scan where you are generally in terms of active/passive control-taking style and vulnerability. If your active control score is 5 and your passive control score is 7, you are somewhere between Tessa Terrified and Oliver Ostrich. If you have a strong toughness number (such as − 90) and a very high active control factor (over 7), you would be close to Charles Atlas. If your passive control figure is 7 or higher and your toughness (vulnerability) number is − 80, you're going to be getting very near Sarah Slug. And so forth.

Your Control-Taking Style *(concluded)*

Your Vulnerability Assessment

Tough as nails	− 100	Impervious
	− 75	
Think you have nine lives	− 50	

	− 25	
Tough and Tender	0	Balanced
	25	

Tenderfoot	50	
	75	
Tender as a baby's bottom	100	Vulnerable

If you are a Tessa Terrified type, you tend to feel highly vulnerable to outside people and things, and try to cope with that feeling by overreacting. You probably would buy too much insurance and be susceptible to any kind of sales pitch. You need to recognize that this style is extreme and leaves you susceptible to being victimized by an overzealous insurance agent.

If you resemble Charles Atlas on this chart, you like to be in charge of any situation, but may tend to underestimate the power of natural disasters, uncontrollable accidents, and just plain lousy luck. You are probably underinsured.

If your score is near Oliver Ostrich, you may feel terribly vulnerable to the outside world, but don't know what to do about it. So you hide your head and hope nothing will happen or somebody will take care of things for you. You may have insurance, but chances are it's the wrong kind, unless your agent cares more for you than most agents would.

If you find yourself somewhere around Sarah Slug's square, and haven't a worry in the world, you may be okay if you have a keeper, but you could be heading for trouble if you don't shape up and start looking out for yourself.

Very likely you will not land directly in any of the corners with these colorful people, but will be somewhere in the middle. If you do end up matched with one of them, though, consider it lucky that you are now more aware of your association with this kind of decision-making character.

	Vulnerability	
	+50 or higher	*−50 or lower*
Active Control (7 or higher)	Tessa Terrified	Charles Atlas
Passive Control (7 or higher)	Oliver Ostrich	Sarah Slug

Property: What Does It Mean to You?

Wealth and possessions, or lack thereof, determine our lifestyles, how we perceive ourselves, how we perceive others, how others perceive us, and the decisions we make. Of course all this reflects our values at any given time, but why we do what we do is very much affected by what we have.

It may be said that money and property make not just for personal but for social power. It has always been said that money can't buy happiness and vice versa. Let's consider those ideas in terms of our sense of social identity and the control we wield over that identity (social status) through protection of our possessions.

The supposed conflict between human rights and property rights has been a constant point of contention in our society. There are those at one end of the spectrum who believe that all property should be divided among all people. At the other end of the spectrum are those who are convinced that the only reliable foundation of personal freedom is the financial security of owning property.

Our reason for bringing this up has nothing to do with politics or social justice. It has a lot to do with our social needs and sense of social identity being all wrapped up together. It is this area we need to probe and sort through before thinking about specific insurance decisions.

Replacement Value

In every society from the beginning of civilization, people have categorized each other as superior or inferior by assigning more importance to some than to others. Criteria may include occupation, race, religion, education, and certainly property and wealth.

People low on the social scale tend to feel far less control over their lives than those who are higher. The person who tries to improve his or her social status may find that the next rung on the ladder is slippery, making it difficult to climb higher. At the same time it is very stressful to drop lower. Slipping could cause a loss of self-esteem and a feeling of worthlessness. This is the primary reason for protecting what is already yours.

Speaking of your property, the amount of insurance you buy for that property should be determined by how you value it, personally, and whether you would replace it if it were gone. In terms of insuring your life and health, you must think in a similar way, except to substitute their replacement (which is, of course impossible) with how much your dependents would need in order to maintain or improve their current status if you were not around.

So once again, before making any financial protection decisions, it is important for you to scrutinize how you feel. Do it on paper so you will have something to refer to and reflect on. Keep in mind that it is not change, but your reaction to it that determines your needs. If your house burns down, the greatest consideration will not be the loss of those particular nails and boards, but whether your personal security is threatened and to what extent. You will want to know what you should do to reduce that threat.

If you are unfortunate enough to be stricken with a devastating financial loss resulting in emotional turmoil, nothing helps more than to be able to immediately locate documents and information you need for contemplating your next move to reinstate your peace of mind.

Remember, when you update your balance sheet every year, to jot down the fair market value *and* the replacement cost figures to determine what you have now. You will have to decide what you would do if something happened to any of your possessions. Would you replace them, forget them, or get something else that may serve more than just that one purpose? All these considerations play an important role in your ultimate insurance decisions.

To assist you further in discovering just how your social needs may influence your decision-making, we have provided the "Taking Stock, Your Social Needs Profile" self-evaluation on the following pages.

Taking Stock

Your Social Needs Profile

We want to stress that this is not a test, but another device to increase your skills in the decision-making process. Your needs will change as your accomplishments and goals advance, so this information will not be set in cement, but will be interesting to check over five years, or even one year, from now. To determine your profile, choose the one alternative that best fits how you feel about the situation in each of the ten questions below and circle the letter in front of that choice. When you have finished the questionnaire, see the evaluation on the next page for information on scoring and interpreting your answers.

---

1. If I had one wish, it would be for
   a. happiness.
   b. a wonderful family life.
   c. all the money I could ever spend.
   d. the respect of my colleagues.

2. I couldn't love somebody unless that person
   a. accepted me just as I am for better or worse.
   b. loved me too.
   c. had the same need to succeed in life that I have.
   d. was attractive and successful.

Your Social Needs Profile *(continued)*

3. If somebody else got the promotion I expected
  a. it would cause me great anxiety and terrible depression.
  b. I'd be ashamed to tell anybody.
  c. I would look for another job with a higher salary.
  d. I would hate to tell my family members and upset them.

4. The way I appear to others
  a. is the last thing I think about.
  b. means something to me, but not much.
  c. is their problem if they worry about it.
  d. is very important to me.

5. I am most impressed with people who
  a. seem to be content with themselves.
  b. have happy families and good friends.
  c. are financially independent.
  d. have the ability to lead others.

6. I am most annoyed with people who
  a. are phonies.
  b. are disloyal to their friends or families.
  c. don't even try to succeed in life.
  d. don't seem to care about anything I do or think.

7. I am
  a. a philosopher.
  b. a lover.
  c. an entrepreneur.
  d. a team player.

8. When I was a child and dreamed of being grown up, I imagined myself as being
  a. smiling and happy.
  b. loved by a wonderful person.
  c. rich and successful.
  d. popular.

9. If anything major changed in my life unexpectedly, I would probably
  a. be excited about what would happen next.
  b. first check to see how my family was dealing with it.
  c. make sure I wasn't going to lose anything in the process.
  d. check with my friends and colleagues to see how they might handle the situation.

10. The position that a politician takes on an issue should be determined by
  a. what he or she thinks is best.
  b. what's best for his or her family and associates.
  c. what will get him or her elected.
  d. what the majority of the populace thinks.

Evaluating Your Social Needs Profile

The inventory that follows was designed to reflect your needs in four areas. The (a) alternatives reflect a need for psychological well-being, the need for per-

---

Your Social Needs Profile (concluded)

---

sonal satisfaction and contentment. The (b) alternatives reflect your need to love others and be loved by them, as well as the need to be sure your loved ones are secure. If you marked many (c) alternatives, you are highly motivated by the need to be successful, and worldly goods are very important to you. If you circled many (d) options, you need to be thought well of by others and value outside opinions highly.

Count the number of choices you made for each alternative, (a), (b), (c), and (d), and circle the total for each on the chart below. This inventory was designed so you cannot get very high scores on all the scales. Rather, it was designed so you can see what values and needs are *most* important to you and refer back to see how you have changed over time.

Inventory of Needs/Values

A Psychological Well-Being	B Family/Love	C Material Possessions	D Social Acceptance
10	10	10	10
9	9	9	9
8	8	8	8
7	7	7	7
6	6	6	6
5	5	5	5
4	4	4	4
3	3	3	3
2	2	2	2
1	1	1	1

Everyone has social needs and desires for material things. Those needs and desires vary from person to person. Most people just go along doing, never stopping to think about how they feel about the parts of themselves that just seem built in. If you take the time to think about these things in a personal way, you will have an advantage in planning and getting appropriate protection for yourself and your family. Nobody will be able to sell you the Brooklyn Bridge unless you think it would really add to your backyard and your social self-esteem!

WRAPPING UP

Now that you know everything you always thought you didn't want to know about insurance, let's review briefly. First, you are now aware that there are a great many misconceptions about what kinds of coverage you should or should not have, why you should have it, and for how long. At the same time, we hope you have been impressed with the fact that burglar alarms and double-bolt locks, though important, will never take the place of proper insurance in protecting your belongings.

For this reason, you should pay serious attention to making sure you fully understand what you are buying and the service you are getting. An attentive agent is vital to proper service. That agent's relationship to the insurance company is paramount to that service, especially in the event of a claim.

Second, you have taken stock of your feelings and personal needs concerning what you own and your environment. You certainly will never again shop for insurance with emotions blazing on your sleeve. You will shop objectively and often, as your policy terms end or your needs change.

A good plan is a flexible plan. There is absolutely no need to become premium poor in order to be adequately protected. *Insurance is to shield your finances in case of a disaster. It is not for banking or increasing your assets.* Invest on your own, never through an insurance company.

We have enjoyed writing this book for you. We sincerely hope that it has served and will continue to serve you well. The other books in the One Hour Guide series are written with the same intention: to help you grow by taking control of your financial life.

APPENDIX

ACTION PAPERS

Action Paper No. 1

Shopping for Auto Insurance

Current Insurer _____

Renewal date _____

	Current Insurer	Prospective Insurer 1	Prospective Insurer 2

	Limits		Premium*
	Car 1	Car 2	
Public liability			
Bodily injury			
Property damage			
Medical expenses (no-fault)			
Uninsured motorist protection			
Physical damage			
Comprehensive			
Deductible			
Collision			
Deductible			
Total annual premium			

*Total premium for coverage area, regardless of number of cars.

Action Paper No. 2

Your Personal Property Inventory

Article Category	1 Number of Articles	2 Total Original Cost	3 Average Age (years)	4 Annual Depreciation	5 Total Depreciation	6 Today's Cost	7 Accumulated Dollar Depreciation	8 Market Value
TOTAL								

Action Paper No. 3

Shopping for Property Insurance

Policy type _____

Current Insurer _____

Renewal date _____

		Current Insurer	Prospective Insurer 1	Prospective Insurer 2
	Limits	**Premiums**		
Home				
Detached buildings				
Trees, shrubs, plants				
Personal property on premises				
Personal property off premises				
Additional living expenses				
Comprehensive personal liability				
Medical expense payments				
Scheduled items				
Endorsements				
Extended theft				
Inflation protection				
Replacement cost				
Full measure plus				
Other (e.g., earthquake, flood)				
Deductible				
Total annual premium				

┌───┐

Action Paper No. 4

Statement of Income Disability Needs

Name _____

Date _____

1. Annual living expenses $ _____

2. Adjusted annual living expenses

    Tax savings $ _____

    Insurance premiums waived   _____

    Other _____   _____

3. Spouse's income   _____

4. Investment income   _____

5. Social Security benefits   _____

6. Total Adjustments (2 + 3 + 4 + 5) $ _____

7. Net annual disability income needs (1−6) $ _____

└───┘

Action Paper No. 5

Shopping for Health Insurance

Medical expense coverage	Insurer 1	Insurer 2	Insurer 3
Company	_____	_____	_____
Limits	_____	_____	_____
Hospital maximum	$ _____	$ _____	$ _____
Surgical maximum	$ _____	$ _____	$ _____
Home health care	$ _____	$ _____	$ _____
Physician care	$ _____	$ _____	$ _____
Psychiatric care (including alcohol and drug rehabilitation)	$ _____	$ _____	$ _____
Major medical maximum	$ _____	$ _____	$ _____
Deductible	$ _____	$ _____	$ _____
Co-payment provisions	_____	_____	_____
Stop-loss limit	$ _____	$ _____	$ _____
Annual premium	$ _____	$ _____	$ _____
Exclusions	_____	_____	_____
Dental coverage			
Deductible	$ _____	$ _____	$ _____
Co-payment provisions	_____	_____	_____
Exclusions	_____	_____	_____
Disability income coverage			
Company	_____	_____	_____
Monthly benefits			
Total disability	$ _____	$ _____	$ _____
Partial disability	$ _____	$ _____	$ _____
Maximum age			
Accident	_____	_____	_____
Illness	_____	_____	_____
Waiting period	_____	_____	_____
Annual premium	$ _____	$ _____	$ _____

Action Paper No. 6

The Eight-Step Procedure

Name(s) _____

Date _____

1. Funeral, administrative, and estate tax expenses $ _____

2. Debt resolution (excluding home mortgage)   _____

3. Contingency fund (twice your monthly take-home pay)   _____

4. College fund   _____

5. **Net Annual Living Expenses**

   a. Average annual living expenses   _____

   b. Spouse's average annual income $ _____

   c. Average annual Social Security   _____

   d. Net annual income needs (a - b - c)   _____

   e. Years until spouse reaches age 90   _____

   f. Average annual investment rate factor (Table 6-1)   _____

   g. Total Net Income Needs (d × f) $ _____

6. Total Monetary Needs (1 + 2 + 3 + 4 + 5g) $ _____

7. Total Investment Assets $ _____

8. Your life insurance needs (**6 - 7**) $ _____

INDEX

A

A. M. Best & Company, 97
American Council of Life Insurance, 82
Auto accident procedure, 36-38
Auto insurance
  bodily injury and property damage,
    26-27
  cancellation clause, 24-26
  collision coverage, 28
  comprehensive coverage, 28
  financial responsibility laws, 26
  jacket and coverage provisions, 24-26
  medical expense coverage, 27-28,
    30-32
  no-fault laws and, 24
  physical property damage coverage,
    28, 29-30
  types illustrated, 25
  uninsured motorist coverage, 26, 30,
    32-33
Auto insurance rates
  age and, 33
  assigned risk plans, 35-36
  discount check list, 35
  distances driven and, 34
  good student program, 34
  safe driver plans, 33

B

BB&K Rule-of-Three, 9-10
(A. M.) Best & Company, 97

B

Best's Insurance Reports, 12, 97
Best's Review, 99
Blue Cross and Blue Shield, 16, 63
Buying disability insurance
  major suppliers, 73
  reading the fine print, 73
  understanding the clauses, 74
Buying insurance policies, 11-12
  agent types, 12-13
  comparing policies, 97-100
  indexes, 99
  rating companies, 12
  use of yellow pages, 11

C

Cash value insurance, 92-94
Coinsurance clause, 46-47
  coverage limits, 46
  replacement cost, 46
Comprehensive liability insurance
  choices of policies illustrated, 20
  determining amounts of needed cover-
    age, 21-22
  financial visibility, 19
  general liability coverage, 22-24
  understanding liability exposure,
    18-21
Comprehensive medical expense coverage, 63
Condominium-unit owners coverage, 52
Contingent beneficiaries, 101
Coverage provisions, 14, 23, 24-26

D

Dealing with insurance agents, 12-13
Death benefit settlement options, 104-6
Deductibles, 9-10
    added savings quotient (ASQ), 9-10
    in auto insurance, 29
    BB&K Rule-of-Three, 9
    in homeowners policies, 51
    in medical coverage, 59
Deposit term insurance, 92
Disability insurance
    basic contracts, 69
    determining your needs, 71-73
    industrial policies, 70
    limited contracts, 70
    scheduled disability income illustrated,
        69
    self-insuring for income loss, 68
    statement of disability income needs il-
        lustrated, 72
    temporary disability insurance (TDI),
        73
    types of clauses, 74-76
Duplication of coverage, 77

E-F

Endowment policies, 94
Federal Emergency Management Agency
    (FEMA), 53
Fee-for-service medical plans, 60
Fee-for-service providers, 63-65
Financial planning, 40, 80
Financial statements, 7
Financial visibility, 40
Floaters, 53
Flood and earthquake insurance, 53-54

G-H

Group health insurance, 76-77
Health expense associations, 16
Health insurance check list, 80
Health Maintenance Act of 1973, 63

Health Maintenance Organizations
    (HMOs), 65
    advantages of belonging to, 66
    types of, 65
Homeowners or renters policy, 43,
    49-52
    condominium-unit owners coverage, 52
    declining deductible, 51
    deductible clauses, 51
    limits on stolen valuables, 49
    package policies, 49
    personal property in transit, 49
    types of, 50-52
House of Commons in England, 5

I

Indemnity plans, 59-60
Inflation, 48, 58, 73
Inflation guard policies, 48
Insurable risks, 4-6
Insurance coverage and financial success, 1
Insurance Information Inc., 100
Insurance policy as legal contract, 13-14
    coverage provisions, 14
    endorsements, 14
    jacket provisions, 14
Insurance principles
    amounts of insurance to carry, 17
    becoming the expert, 2
    buying a policy, 11-12
    cutting through jargon, 2
    dealing with agents, 12-13
    dealing with risks, 6
    determinig how long to keep coverage,
        10-11
    explanation of, 5
    four P's of insurance, 4
    insurable risks, 4
    making the insurance decision, 7
    paying premiums, 14-15
    prioritizing needs, 8
    transferring risk, 17
Inventory of needs/values, 120
Investable assets, 73

J-L

Jacket provisions, 13-14, 22, 24-26
Legal liability, 40
Length of time to keep insurance, 10-11
Liability and auto insurance check list, 39
Liability exposure, 18-21
    and determining needed coverage, 21
    financial visibility, 19
    types of 20-21
Life insurance as an investment, 100, 107
Life insurance needs, 81-88, 103-4, 106
    changing circumstances and, 86-88
    comparison shopping and, 106
    contract clauses, 101-3
    customizing policies to fit, 103-4
    eight-step approach for determining, 83-86
    net worth and balance sheet, 83
    Social Security and, 85
Limited payment life, 93
Lloyd's of London, 16-17

M

Major medical insurance, 60-63
    automatic restoration clause, 62
    coinsurance feature, 62
    stop-loss-limit, 62
Making a claim, 36-37, 55-56
Market value, 42
Medical coverage, 78
Medical insurance, 58-63
    determining needs, 58
    personal balance sheet, 59
    types of plans, 60
Medicare, 67
Medicare supplementary insurance, 67
Mortgage term insurance, 92
Mutual companies, 16

N-O

National Association of Insurance Commissioners, 97

National Insurance Consumer Organization, 97
Ordinary life insurance, 93

P

Package policies, 52
Personal Articles Floater, 43
Personal balance sheet, 59
Personal property inventory, 44-45
    as documentation, 44
    illustrated, 45
    substantiating a claim, 44
Preferred Provider Organizations (PPOs), 66
Premium payment clause, 102
Premiums, 14-15, 89
Pre-paid medical plans, 60
Prepayment plans, 59
Price and market values, 42
Primary beneficiary, 101
Property
    improvements to, 48
    personal, 41
    real, 41
    and social identity, 117
Property insurance
    effect of inflation on, 47
    insurable classifications, 41
    personal property inventory, 44
    role of, 41
    selecting the right coverage, 48-55
    tips on saving money, 57

R

Replacement cost, 42, 46
    and consumer price index, 48
    and geographic areas, 47
    and inflation, 47
    and market value, 42
Replacement cost coverage, 42, 43, 46
Replacement cost endorsement, 43, 47
Replacement value, 117

S

Single-premium life insurance policies, 100
Social needs profile, 118-20
Social Security, 71, 76, 79, 85
Stock companies, 16
Straight life insurance, 93
Suicide prevention clause, 103

T

Taking stock questionnaire, 112-13
Tax Reform Act of 1986, 100
Temporary disability insurance (TDI), 73
Term insurance, 89-92
  decreasing term, 91
  deposit, 92
  guaranteed rate, 90
  guaranteed renewable coverage, 90
  level term, 91
  mortgage, 92
Term versus cash value life insurance, 96-97
Types of insurance companies, 15-17

Types of property insurance coverage, 48-49

U

Umbrella liability policies, 23
Underlying principle of insurance, 5, 18, 41
Understanding the fine print, 55
Understanding yourself, 108-10
Universal life insurance, 94-95

V

Valuing your home, 46
Variable life insurance, 95-96
Variables in life insurance policies, 88-89
Vulnerability quotient, 113, 115

W-Y

Wealth and possessions, 117
Whole life insurance, 93
Workers compensation, 79
Your control-taking personality, 111